SO YOU WANT TO BE A LEADER

Steven Wakefield

DEDICATION

I would like to dedicate this book to my wife Fran. Fran has worked tirelessly in helping me achieve so much in my working life. Without Fran's support this book would never have been written. A huge thank you to my daughter Kirsty for some inspiring ideas while I was writing this book.

Lots of love,

Steven Wakefield

Table of Contents

Chapter 1

Leadership

This book has been written to help those people who either aspire to be a leader or are leading a group of people and want to understand how to strengthen and build their relationship with their team.

What is the difference between being a manager and being a leader? Can you be a leader without being a manager? It is said that to be a leader is to "do the right things" and to be a manager is "to do things right". Your organisation expects managers to follow processes, for example, planning, designing, and creating tasks for your team so that they can deliver excellence. Being a leader means that you need to understand, empathise and motivate your team towards goals to which you are all committed. It means to fully understand peoples' point of view and being flexible enough to consider their views when making any decision. However, being a leader does not just mean you lead people. Being a leader also entails a mindset that challenges current thinking and current processes and procedures. Leading also means continually educating yourself in both your business and personal life. Being a thought leader is just as important as being a leader of people. A thought leader is a person who is aware of all the latest trends in their chosen subject. A thought leader is a person or organisation who is at the forefront of their chosen topic, and it is a person that people will go to if they want to gain further insight into a subject.

In essence, a leader is someone who has a strategic role, ensuring that the ship is in the right ocean and they are helping to guide the ship towards the correct port.

Some companies and organisations have exemplary Human Resource processes and procedures that they follow when they appoint a new manager whether that is internally or externally. However, the focus is often related to the organisation's operations, whereas the first objective should be to look at the core values of the organisation. What does the organisation stand for, what is the organisation trying to achieve? Understanding these values will lead to employing people who have the same values and drive that the organisation has.

Many organisations have a well thought out Mission Statement that was developed or agreed by well-meaning Board members. The Mission Statement indicates the company's values and its commitment to those values. However, how many people have contributed to the Mission Statement? Usually, only a few people were involved. Often decisions regarding Mission Statements are part of a marketing exercise. The value of a Mission Statement is something that will be viewed by suppliers and potential customers; it will give them a clear indication of your company values. However, a Mission Statement could be more than this. As a leader, it is vital to understand both your company's and your Mission Statements. These are the core values that you hold dear. Every action you take should be with the Mission Statements in mind. Therefore, you need to understand who you are and what your company stands for before you can begin the journey to being a respected leader.

Often when we accept a managerial or leadership role, we focus on the technical aspects of the job. The technical understanding of your position is fundamental to your success, but there are other skills that you will need to gain respect and demonstrate to your team that you are their leader.

In the definition of Leadership, there is one small word which needs some clarification. That word is "ability". The leader should have the ***ability*** to lead a team or organisation. However, what does “ability” mean? There are skills that leaders need that are just as important as the technical aspect of the role, some of which are:

1. Understanding Who You Are – Without knowing who you are and how you react to situations, and without knowing what your management style is, and how people perceive you it is challenging to lead others successfully.
2. Training, Coaching and Mentoring – How do you manage people? Do you have one method for everyone in your team or do you have a plan for each person? How do you help your team to progress? Do you have a mentor?
3. Goal Setting – Do you set Goals for yourself and your team? How do you monitor the Goals? Goal setting with accountability can dramatically improve your team's productivity.
4. Decision Making – Have you considered how your thought process work? How do you make decisions?
5. Critical Thinking – Do you asses each critical decision you make by reviewing all the facts or do you decide based on your past experiences?
6. Speaking – How you communicate with people is vital. However, speaking only accounts for around 40% of what we communicate; approximately 10% is the words that we use, and 30% is in the tone and inclination.
7. Words We Use – The words we use and how and when we use them are critical. How do you greet your team, your customers or your potential customers? How do you start meetings?

8. Body Language – Body language accounts for about 60% of what we communicate to the people around us. Do you understand how your eyes, face, arms, hand and posture give out powerful signals?
9. Active Listening – Have you thought of your response before the person you are speaking to has finished their point? Do you practice your listening skills?
10. Questioning techniques – Asking "Who, What, Why, When", along with open and closed questions helps you understand the other person's viewpoint. The way you question situations can have a fundamental effect on how you are perceived.
11. Mindfulness – Are you too busy to focus on the things that are important to you, the team, and your business or organisation? Do you take time to understand the people, issues and circumstances that you have to deal with each day?
12. Stress – Stress can be good for you and your team, but too much pressure can break your team. How do you cope with stress? How does your organisation deal with stress?
13. At Play – It is essential that you have time off; otherwise, you will be far less effective. If you want to be more productive resting and doing something you enjoy outside of the work environment is vital. How do you relax?
14. Learning and Education – What time do you put aside for your education? Great leaders are always looking for an opportunity to learn.

Most people will take on a leadership role sometime in their working lives whether it is leading an organisation, a department, a team, a project or organising an event. Often, we are given a role with more responsibility if we have demonstrated that we are good at our present job. There are many occasions when this leads to the "Peter Principle" which was initially observed by Laurence J Peter. The principle was later published in the book "The Peter

Principle" by Peter and Raymond Hull. The Peter Principle means career progression stops when you find a role that is beyond your capabilities. As an example, somebody who is excellent at coding is then asked to run a small project, which means that their programming experience is still relevant which results in a successful project. The next stage is to be asked to run a more significant project and again the programming experience and running a small project is relevant. Then you are asked to run a large team at which point the programming experience is mostly irrelevant. Instead, man management is the primary role, and this is where the Peters Principle can come into effect. Have you the skills to be a good man manager? A good leader will recognise that they have some weaknesses and will put a plan together to mitigate the risks that they have identified. However, all too often we are left to struggle through.

As you can see becoming a leader is much more than doing your job well. You may well be the best person for the technical aspects of your role, but if you want to gain respect as a leader, you will need to start to look at yourself far more in-depth than you have done in the past. Are you ready for that challenge?

Chapter 2

Understanding Who You Are

Do you know who you are? A strange question but if you don't understand what makes you tick, how your past experiences influence your decisions and how your peers and colleagues see your behaviours then becoming a good leader will be a bit hit and miss.

Decision Making and Your Belief System

As individuals, the survival instinct is one of the few things that we inherit when we are born. From then on, we learn our behaviours and values from our parents, family, family friends, friends, peer group, teachers, community and the media. In today's world, we are overwhelmed by other people's views of the world.

When we are looking at a problem or issue, our subconscious mind will look at all the "facts" and offer a decision based on our belief system. Therefore if you see people "jump to a conclusion" before the presentation of all the facts, you will see their belief system at work.

Every day we have decisions to make and how we make those decisions is based on our experience. Our subconscious brain takes in all the data then reviews our experience in similar situations and decides what the outcome should be. The conscious part of the brain reacts if there is something that is out of the ordinary or if something challenges our view in some way. By understanding who we are we start to know what influences us and why we react as we do.

Intelligence Quotient and Emotional Quotient

There are two significant ways of assessing your intelligence, that is by your Intelligence Quotient (IQ) and your Emotional Quotient (EQ). Most organisation employ people based on their IQ. The IQ test is a way of measuring short-term memory, analytical thinking, language skills, mathematical ability and spatial recognition along with problem-solving skills. There is a great deal of emphasis put into IQ as this taken as an indicator of people's intelligence. However, it is not a guarantee of greatness or leadership ability. Many people have a high IQ but struggle to lead. The reason is that they lack EQ. The EQ is a measure of peoples' ability to empathise with people around them. It is the ability to understand your own emotions and the emotions of those around you. The better your EQ, the better you will appreciate people around you, and the more comfortable you will find it to lead people.

EQ is something that you can work on improving every day. EQ is being self-aware, knowing why you are behaving the way you are, and understanding why you are making the decisions you are making. EQ is having the listening skills, the ability to ask meaningful questions and listening with an empathetic ear. EQ is the ability to respond to situations calmly rather than reacting to those issues. In short, EQ is using our emotions to connect to people positively. These are all skills that are not so easy to measure, and yet if you develop them, it is incredible how positively your colleagues perceive you.

Personality Types

We all have a "personality type" C. J. Jung theorised that there are four distinct groups with two opposite preferences in each group.

The four groups lead to sixteen different personalities. The four groups are:

- Favourite World – Do you focus on your inner world or the outer world? How you focus is called or Introversion (I) or Extraversion (E)
- Information - Do you focus on the basic information or do you prefer to interpret the information and add to it? How you deal with information is called Sensing (S) or Intuition (I)
- Decisions – When you make a decision do you initially look at logic and consistency or do you first look at the people and special circumstances? How you make decisions is called Thinking (T) or Feeling (F).
- Structure – When you deal with the outside world, do you prefer to decide on things or do you prefer to stay open to new information and options? How you deal with the outside world is called Judging (J) or Perceiving (P).

The Myers & Briggs Foundation - Mbti® Basics, https://www.myersbriggs.org/my-mbti-personality-type/mbti-basics (accessed March 31, 2019).

The sixteen groups are:

ISTJ	ISFJ	INFJ	INTJ
ISTP	ISFP	INFP	INTP
ESTP	ESFP	ENFP	ENTP
ESTJ	ESFJ	ENFJ	ENTJ

There are sites such as www.16personalities.com that provide free tests to assess your personality type.

Here is a brief description of each personality type that the website gives:

Analytical:

INTJ

An Advocate – Imaginative and Strategic thinkers

INTP

A Logician – Innovative inventors with a thirst for knowledge

ENTJ

A Commander – Bold, imaginative strong-willed leaders who will always find a way.

ENTP

A Debater – Smart, curious thinkers who cannot resist an intellectual challenge.

Diplomatic:

INFJ

An Advocate – Quiet and mystical, yet very inspiring

INFP

A Mediator – Poetic, kind and altruistic who is always helping a good cause.

ENFJ

A Protagonist – Charismatic and inspiring leaders.

ENFJ

A Campaigner – Enthusiastic, creative and sociable free spirits who generally finds a reason to smile.

Sentinel:
ISTJ

A Logistician – Practical and fact-minded individuals

ISFJ

A Defender – Very dedicated and warm protectors

ESTJ

An Executive – Excellent and administrators, unsurpassed at managing things and people.

ESFJ

A Consul – Extraordinary caring, social and popular, always eager to help

Explorer:
ISTP

A Virtuoso – Bold, practical experimenters, masters of all types of tools

ISFP

An Adventurer – Flexible and charming artists, always ready to explore and experience something new

ESTP

An Entrepreneur – Smart, energetic and very perspective who enjoys living on the edge

ESFP

An Entertainer – Spontaneous, energetic and enthusiastic people who are always fun to be around

The Wheel of Business Life

Have you planned out your career? Is each step moving you towards your goal? Alternatively, are you like most people who set out on life's journey with little idea of where they want to go, how they will get there or what they will do when you finally arrive. It is like getting on a sailboat at the beginning of a journey without enough training, a map, a sail, an engine or any idea of the tides and winds that you will encounter. You will only become a successful leader by luck.

How do we become a leader without relying on luck? We must first look at ourselves. Where are we right now? Below is the "Wheel of Business Life", this shows our current view of the world. The original concept was created by Paul J. Meyer, founder of Success Motivation® Institute, Inc.

WHEEL OF BUSINESS LIFE

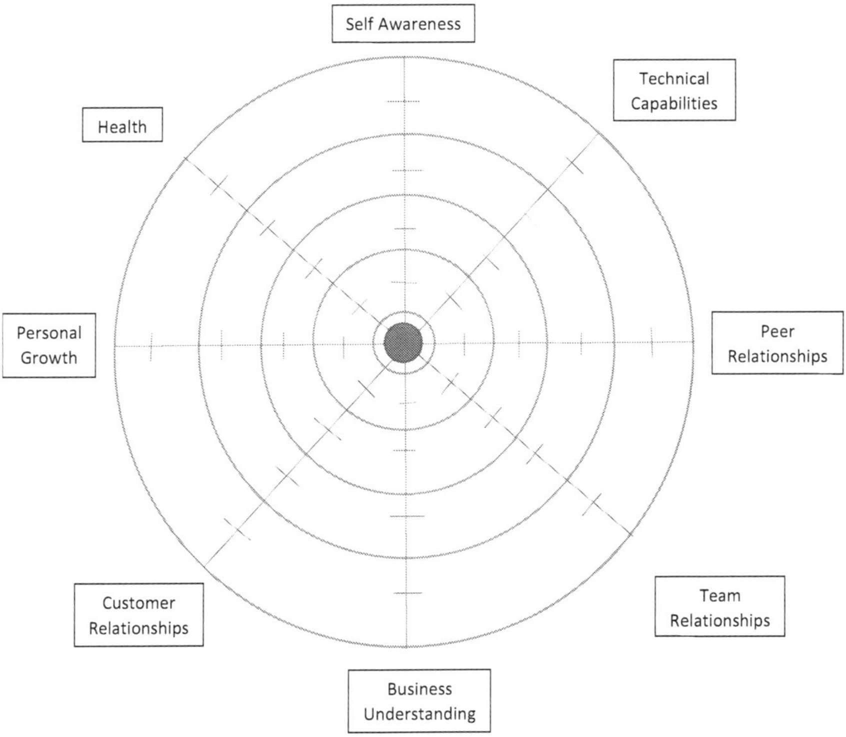

COMPLETE THE WHEEL:

1. **Review the 8 Wheel Categories -** think briefly what a satisfying life might look like for you in each area.
2. **Next, draw a line across each segment that represents your satisfaction score as of today for each area.**

- Imagine the centre of the wheel is 0 and the outer edge is 10
- Choose a value between 1 (very dissatisfied) and 10 (fully satisfied)

You are in the centre of the wheel. The centre represents where you are the weakest, and the outer circle represents where you are strongest. By putting an "x" on the corresponding point of the circle and then joining up the "x" points, you will start to understand where you feel you are about all the other things going on in your business life.

Self-Awareness. How self-aware are you? Do you review your business life and reflect on your role, your relationships and your career prospects? Do you understand how your decision-making process works? Do you do this regularly? Remember this is an honest look at where you are without any judgement.

Technical Capabilities – being up-to-date on the technical aspects of your role is essential. Being able to make decisions based on the most up-to-date information related to your field will significantly enhance the trust your team will have in you.

Peer Relationships – How do your directors, managers and peers view you? How do you see them? Do you have a good working relationship with all the key people in your organisation? How are your networking skills?

Team Relationships –Does your team work well under pressure? Would they come to you if they have issues inside or outside work? If each member of the group were to give you an appraisal of your role what would the outcome be?

Business Understanding – Do you have a good understanding of how your business works? How do you measure your success against your competitors? What is your company or organisation strategy? Is the strategy in the Business Plan just words on paper or do you believe in the strategy? Do you champion the approach? How does that relate to your team? If asked could you give a 10-minute presentation about your business and your key customers, and how your part of the organisation offers real benefits and value to both your business and customers?

Customer Relationships – Who are your key customers? Who benefits from working with you and your team? Why do they prefer working with you rather than one of your competitors? Do you know any of your customers outside the working environment? What is your customers business? How do they judge success in their business? Who are their main competitors? How do you add value to them? Could your customers give a 10-minute presentation on your business and how you help them meet their customer's needs?

Personal Growth – Have you an individual growth plan? How do you measure your growth? What training do you have planned for the coming year? Does the exercise you are looking at reinforce current skills or add new skills?

Health – If you have health issues you cannot give your best to the team or organisation. Have you a fitness plan? Do you participate in sports activities? How often do you assess your health? How healthy are your team?

Assessing where you are in each of the eight categories will give you an idea of your current strengths and weaknesses. Now it is time to look at how you can build on those strengths and work on the weaknesses. The best way to do this is to set some goals. Chapter 4 Goal Setting will go into detail on how to do this, but you should have a goal that splits into small tasks. Each task should be time-bound and measurable. It is amazing what you can achieve by writing down and committing to your goals.

The point of completing the Business Wheel of Life is to give you an understanding of where you are in respect to your working life. However, that is only the beginning of knowing what drives you. How have you got to your current role?

Belief System

We all have a belief system. The belief system is a set of values that we have built up through our lives. Many of the values that we have are from our parents and the people that brought us up. Have you thought of how that affects you every day? Our parents, community and teachers expect certain behaviours, and while we may rebel at some of those expectations at some time in our lives, we generally come to accept them. What is your work ethic? Were you taught that hard work pays off? Do you respect your elders? Can you hear your parents or grandparents in your head sometimes when you are speaking to members of your team? That is your belief system at work. If you want to start to understand your fundamental values then imagine you are 100 years old and that you are coming to the end of your life, your great-grandchildren are visiting you and you know that you will not see them again. What advice would you give your great grandchildren? How should your great-grandchildren conduct themselves? What would you say was the most important thing they could do with their lives? The advice you would offer is what is at the core of your belief system.

Once we understand how our belief system is affecting our everyday lives, we can look at how we can start to change these automatic processes and attitudes. One of the best ways to do this is to set goals; another is to look deeper into how we make decisions which is a topic in Chapter 10 about Mindfulness. If you combine that with assessing the way you communicate you will have started on the path to be a well-respected leader.

Motivation

However, are you motivated to be a leader?

Motivation is a powerful driver. We are all motivated to improve ourselves in some way. At the most basic level, we are motivated to have warmth, shelter, food and drink. After achieving these basic needs, we look for security, order and stability next we strive for love and belongingness. These are the first three levels of Maslow's Theory of Motivation. Maslow, A. H. (1943). A theory of human motivation. Psychological Review, 50*(4), 370-396.*

Maslow's hierarchy of needs gives us an understanding of how we are motivated to grow. The Maslow Pyramid originally had five levels; some we will achieve naturally but the higher up the pyramid you go, the more you will be work towards those levels. The updated version has seven levels as the initial premise was that you needed to achieve all the elements of each level before you could move to the next level. However, Maslow later concluded that "You only needed to be satisfied that you had completed most of the requirements before your motivation took you the next level". Maslow further stated that "Only around 2% of human beings that have ever lived had achieved Self Actualisation".

The levels are:

1. *Biological and physiological needs* - air, food, drink, shelter, warmth, sex, sleep.
2. *Safety needs* - protection from elements, security, order, law, stability.
3. *Love and belongingness needs* - friendship, intimacy, trust, and acceptance, receiving and giving affection and love. Affiliating, being part of a group (family, friends, work).
4. *Esteem needs* - which Maslow classified into two categories: (i) esteem for oneself (dignity, achievement, mastery, independence) and (ii) the desire for reputation or respect from others (e.g., status, prestige).
5. *Cognitive needs* – knowledge and understanding, curiosity, exploration, need for meaning and predictability.

6. *Aesthetic needs* – appreciation and search for beauty, balance and form.

7. *Self-actualisation needs* - realising personal potential, seeking personal growth and peak experiences.

Where are you in Maslow's Hierarchy of Needs? Seniority in an organisation is no indication of what motivates you. Understanding what drives you will give you an opportunity to set goals and tasks that will help you build to the next level and start to reach your full potential.

Initially, working out where you or one of your team is on the pyramid feels like an academic exercise, but when you start to review everyday situations, you can see the levels in action. If you are feeling unwell, your thirst for knowledge reduces dramatically. Then think about somebody in your team that is having relationship issues; they are motivated to try to resolve those issues, and so the need for mastery in a subject is dramatically reduced. Therefore, you will see a drop in their performance.

As a leader, it is not only essential to know where you are on this Hierarchy but to understand where each of your team and your peers are within Maslow's Hierarchy of Needs. Knowing this will mean that you will be able to choose goals and tasks that are likely to motivate them the most. Is someone is looking for status (level 4) or are they thirsting for knowledge (level 5)? Remember what drives you does not necessarily drive each member of your team, some members may well be happy with the level they have reached in the organisation, for example, they will not find motivation with the idea of being promoted or being given more responsibility. They will, however, be motivated when presented with a challenge that means they will need to acquire more knowledge. Understanding this will provide you with a far better insight into your team and peers.

Understanding yourself: Some simple Exercises to help.

There are some exercises that you can do to start to understand yourself. The first would be to complete the Wheel of Life. The Wheel of Life gives you an understanding of where you are.

The second exercise would be to write a short 50-word biography. You can use the Wheel of Life as a basis for the bio. The bio should be honest and none judgemental, remember this is for you to view, nobody else.

The third exercise is to look at what drives you. Take a good look at yourself and write down what motivates you. Are you honest, ethical, and hard working? Is status important to you? Are possessions vital to you? Is faith important to you? Is helping people important to you? Is family important to you? Is work important to you? What is the first thing you think of in the morning when you wake up? What keeps you awake at night? What is the last thing you think of when you go to sleep at night? Be honest, remember this is not the person you want to be (that's the next list) it is a list of what drives you now.

The fourth exercise is to write down who you would like to be. Take a look at the first three exercises. The tasks will give you a good idea of who you are and where you are. It may well be that you will discover some uncomfortable truths. Remember not to judge yourself too harshly. Be honest.

As a leader, you will need to look at your aspirations and marry them with your Company's and team's aspirations. What are your Company's goals? Are they reflected in the goals that you have set yourself and your team? Write down your organisation's goals, short term, medium term and long term then map your goals and your team's goals against the Company's objectives. Is there a match or should you review the lists?

So now you have a map of where you are and a good idea of the direction you want to set sail. You are already in a better state of mind than 95% of the population.

Chapter 3

Training, Coaching and Mentoring

As a leader, you need to understand how you are going to enhance the skills of yourself and your team. Getting the best out of yourself, your team and your organisations mean that you need to keep up with the latest processes, techniques and methodologies in your organisation's sector. A primary responsibility of a leader is ensuring your team is up-to-date.

Training, Coaching and Mentoring are essential when you are leading a team. Many organisations offer lots of training, some coaching but only a few have formal mentoring programs.

Training

Offering training courses to your employees' is the usual way of passing on new information. On the completion of the course, the employees are expected to use what they have learnt in their everyday tasks, to the benefit of both themselves and the company. Training is the best way of passing information to the highest number of people. Training has the best impact when the need is to instruct people on new methods and procedures, such as software programs or health and safety requirements.

Coaching

Coaching rather than training is a better approach where there is a need for a change in culture, or there is a need for a fundamental shift in everyday tasks. Coaching can still be offered to the same number of employees as training, but rather than use the teacher-pupil method, the style provided is that of coacher-coached. Coaching is goal focused where specific goals are agreed, and those goals and associated tasks will follow a process to achieve that goal.

There are a variety of coaching methods, and the three that we will focus on are; Dyadic, Team and Group Coaching.

Dyadic Coaching

Dyadic coaching is one-on-one coaching where both parties agree on a goal and set up a process to achieve the goal. A standard method of moving towards that goal is the GROW technique. G stands for Goal, R is the current Reality, O is for Options, and W is the Way forward.

As an example, you could have a **G**oal "To generate an additional ten leads per month." The current **R**eality could be that on average you are generating 20 leads a month and so you will need to generate 35 leads per month an increase of 50%. The **O**ptions that you have include sending offers to your existing customer base, posting a mailshot to customers and potential customers that you have met in the last six months, setting up three extra meeting a week, and attending more marketing events. The **W**ay forward would be to choose the options that would have the best chance of success.

Following the initial coaching meeting, the next process is RE-GROW. The **R** stands for Review, and the **E** is to Evaluate. Using the RE-GROW methodology means that the outcomes from the last coaching session are reviewed; the results are evaluated to see how they pertain to the agreed Goals. The RE-GROW method will reiterate the Goal, which will lead to an updated current Reality, with a review of the Options, and an updated Way forward agreed.

Team Coaching

Team coaching is working with a team of people who usually work closely together. The objective is to agree on a team goal and work together to achieve that goal. A method that can be used to accomplish a team goal is the GROUP technique. G stands for Goal, R stands for current Reality, O is for Options, U is for other people's Understanding, and P is for agreed Processes to proceed.

As an example, you may have a **G**oal "To improve communication within the team". The current **R**eality is that the primary communication method is through email and ad-hoc meetings. There will be a number of **O**ptions which would include newsletters, scheduled meetings, blogs and vlogs, and texts. The team would meet to discuss their **U**nderstanding of the goal and the various options. Having considered all the options, the team would agree on the **P**rocesses that would most likely achieve the Goal.

In our example of improving communication, we would **R**eview the outcomes since the last meeting, **E**valuate if the process was successful, and then we would readdress the **G**oal based on the new information, reassess the current **R**eality, look at the available **O**ptions, ensure that everyone had the same Understanding, and agree on the **W**ay forward.

Group Coaching

Group coaching is bringing together a group of people who do not usually work together. Using Group coaching is best when a company or organisation is planning to go through a significant change. The methodology used is the same as the team coaching which is the GROUP technique.

Groups are naturally resistant to change and therefore when coaching a team or group; it is essential to understand group dynamics. Skilled coaches will communicate a clear agenda and will guide the group through the process. Members of the group may well be reluctant to discuss things that are outside the regular activity of the group or organisation, and this can cause tension within the group. However, it is these tensions that can, and often do, result in developing outstanding outcomes.

There have been many studies on group dynamics and understanding of how and why groups form will help a great deal when setting up a team to complete a goal. The first thing to note is that the team need a common goal. The early communication of the goal needs to be clear, and each member of the group will need to have a clear understanding of their role to achieve it. However, this is not a one-way communication as each member of the team should be able to clearly articulate their position and the value all the other members bring to the project. This common understanding will start to allow the team to bond.

It is natural that the team will splinter into smaller groups. The group split will occur when each identifies commonalities such as whether they are married or single, what sports team they support, there are many reasons small groups form. Paying attention to the groups within the team and introducing new members of the group into the smaller groups will help strengthen your organisation. A typical outcome of small groups forming is that members call for the eviction of those who don't respect the team rules. So, when you are setting up a group, you should look for the different skills, interests and commonalities of all the participants. When you have built a group or team that have diverse beliefs and experiences, as long as you educate each member of your expectations, you will be surprised at how creative and productive the outcome could be.

The use of group coaching is when organisational changes are the main focus. Setting a clear agenda with defined goals is essential. The group will then develop an understanding of how each member fits into the organisation's structure. Setting clear agenda's and establishing clear goals may seem very basic, but it is common for people within the group to have a limited view of how the organisation works.

A coach will have many ways of working with teams or groups. The two main methods are the "expert" which is the selling and telling approach and the "diagnostic" which is the doctor-patient model. There are benefits to each of these methods, which you chose depends on the group and the goals that have you agree. If some experts are part of the group, the experts will tend to dominate the discussion and decisions. A coach will recognise how the experts are overlooking the opinions of the rest of the group and will challenge the experts thinking and raise alternative approaches for the whole group to discuss.

The different coaching environments are not mutually exclusive. There is often a need to have one-on-one coaching when engaged in a team or group coaching exercise. The reason for this is that members of the organisation or group may not be willing to express some of their feelings or concerns in the general meeting. When this occurs offering a one-on-one session can help.

While it is good to have a way of remembering the processes that we use to coach individuals, teams and groups there are times when the methods can be in a different order. For example, when the individual, team or group cannot agree on a goal, then it would be appropriate to look at the current reality. The success of any coaching session or sessions will depend a great deal on the skill of the coach and the commitment of the people receiving the coaching. It is therefore vital that everybody concerned in the coaching sessions is fully committed as without this commitment the group will struggle to bond and therefore will have difficulty in coming to a consensus. A leader would ensure that each team member would be aware of the benefits of the coaching sessions before arranging the meetings.

Some of the benefits of coaching in groups are:

- Appreciation and alignment of individual goals, strengths and values;
- Greater commitment and accountability;
- Development of coaching skills;
- Increased emotional intelligence;
- Leadership development;
- Improved listening and communication;
- Understanding and self-regulation of acceptable group behaviours;
- Improved likelihood of durable changes in behaviour;
- The development of trust and support within the group;
- Constructive conflict resolution;
- Improved systemic awareness of the organisation;
- Prevention of organisational silo formation;
- Knowledge transfer and management;
- Improved group energy levels;
- Creation of high-performance teams; and
- Better organisational results.

Coaching can bring real benefits to any organisation if your organisation is looking to improve productivity or breakthrough into a new market. If your organisation is facing challenges using coaching to discuss new and innovative ideas can bring real positive change.

Mentoring

However, what about mentoring?

The origin of mentoring comes from Greek mythology. Mentor was the name of Telemachus teacher in Homer's *Odyssey.*

Today, mentoring is the pairing of an experienced person with a junior colleague. It is not considered training as mentoring is not as structured and has no set agenda. The purpose is to help the junior colleague gain from the experience of the mentor. The result is to help improve the junior colleague's performance and productivity at a far superior rate than would normally be expected. The consequence will be a better functioning and more productive organisation.

Does your organisation have a formal mentoring program? If not, why not if the result is a more productive organisation? Is this something that you could bring to your organisation?

Mentors have a lot to gain from their involvement because they must keep up-to-date with the latest trends and activities to be able to make their experience relevant.

A mentor should have five essential qualities:

1. Ability and willingness to communicate
2. People focused
3. Ability to listen
4. Curiosity and inquisitiveness
5. Objectivity and fairness

However, from an everyday practical point of view what is the meaning of being mentored? Do you mentor individuals within your team? Do you have a mentor? Often a quick chat on some impending issue is seen as mentoring. However, mentoring is far more than that. Mentoring is semi-structured; in that, there is a regular meeting with a formal process as well as informal discussions on what the advice the mentee needs.

A mentor, therefore, needs to have specific skills, namely, to be an excellent listener and to be able to question the mentee's assumptions. A good listener is an active listener who has no preconceptions of where the conversation is going to go. Most people have already prepared their next question before the person who is speaking has finished explaining their point. The result of this approach is to instruct not to mentor. Imagine a right-handed drummer trying to teach a left-handed drummer how to play. If you tell the drummer how you play the drums, the likely result would be a disaster. However, by taking a different approach and listening to how the drums are being played and then discussing how the beat is being heard would end with a far better result.

How should you approach mentoring? The first and most obvious thing is for both parties to like one another and they must be able to meet regularly. It is best to have a scheduled time to get together. With today's technology that does not mean you have to be in the same room.

The frequency of formal meetings can vary. Most successful programs advise on one formal meeting per month. The meeting should have a process to begin and end. Typically, the opening should be to discuss any action points from the previous session.

Once you have discussed any action points that were taken since the last meeting a great way of moving on to the next part is to ask what the mentee what they would like to discuss. If there is no specific topic or topics that come to mind, then ask for three positive things that have happened and three negative things that have occurred since the last meeting. The purpose of this is to identify the challenges that the junior colleague has encountered. The objective is to centre the discussion around one, or all of these issues. It is incredible how powerful this approach is.

The mentor should be "people focused" being able to empathise with the mentee. As mentioned, two of the critical qualities that both parties should develop is the ability to be both curious and inquisitive. By having an open and none judgmental approach to the discussions, the outcome of any conversation will be more productive. Curiosity means trying to gain a deeper understanding of the reasons for decisions. What were the circumstances? What was happening at the same time? Who else was involved? Why was the decision required then? How did you feel when you made the decision? What was the outcome? What would you do differently next time?

At the end of the meeting, you should always agree to some action points. These action points will form the basis of the following meeting.

Mentoring can be very powerful and help boost productivity within an organisation. If you don't already have such a program, what have you got to lose by running a pilot project?

Chapter 4

Goal Setting

Goal setting is important. If you don't have goals how can you judge if you or your team are being successful? Many people say they have goals, but when you ask them to show you their goals and how they measure them, they struggle. Having goals is excellent, but if you have not written them down, they are ineffective. By writing down your goals, committing to them, reviewing them regularly and being accountable for your goals you will start to achieve more than you ever thought possible. A leader will have established their own goals and help their team set their goals, both as a team and individually.

When we are at work performing our daily duties, we can get into a rut which means we start repeating the same actions. The odd thing is because we are creatures of habit, we will repeat the steps, even if they are not productive or successful. Once we have learnt how to complete a task, our subconscious brain takes over, and we go into automatic pilot. Think about learning to drive, at first you are concentrating on the way you are going, how you are holding the steering wheel, what your feet are doing, and this is all before you actually start the car! After a few lessons, things become easier this is because your subconscious is now beginning to perform some of the tasks, which allows the conscious part of your brain to focus on the jobs that require more significant effort. When we are working, the same process applies.

At the beginning of a project or a new job, we focus on all the activities that we need to do to complete the task in hand. Then as we get used to the situation or task the issues we face regularly are dealt with by your subconscious mind without too much conscious thought. The result is that people reach a level of performance that they find it difficult to go beyond and things start to stagnate. The lack of progression is sometimes called the Glass Ceiling which describes an invisible barrier to success. The phrase was initially coined by Management Consultant Marilyn Loden almost 40 years ago. By following a few simple steps, it is possible to break through the Glass Ceiling and stretch yourself which will improve the productivity of you, your team and your company.

When people are asked, "What does it take to be successful"? Most people give a list of the critical things that they need to do to be successful. The issue is that while everybody can list all the things that they need to do to be successful, very few people follow that list. Why is this? The fact is that people tend to search out the more manageable tasks and the tasks that they feel comfortable doing. People are under pressure all the time, and so when they have some spare time, they tend to focus on things that help them relax which means they focus on tasks that are easier to accomplish and are not necessarily relevant to achieving their goals. When under pressure you often observe people answering an email that is not important just because it has just popped into their inbox, or you see them checking their phone for messages on their favourite social media site, rather than making a phone call to a prospective client.

We often see people doing things that are not important and will not help them towards their goals. Why do people procrastinate? Procrastination is the thief of time. Why do we continually find things to do that are not productive? How often have you seen yourself or some of your colleagues chatting at the coffee machine, or find you are checking and answering emails that can wait.

Procrastination stops us from achieving our real potential. We find that we don't reach our targets and life seems to drift past us as if we were in a dream. Having a life without goals is the same as floating along in an ocean and hoping that things will go well. So, when the storms hit you have no map, no engine, no sail and no rudder to help you. In Chapter 2 "Understanding Who You Are" we discovered how we could look at a map so that we know where we are starting from and where we would like to end up. Now is the time to use a rudder, build an engine and unfurl the sails. We do that by setting goals.

Procrastination happens when you, or your team, are not focused or not committed to what you want to achieve. That is why you find yourself drifting from one task to another. By writing down want you to want to achieve and then planning how you will make it, you will focus on what is important to you.

No matter what you want to achieve, there is a way to do it. However, to be successful, you need to plan how you will be successful. Success very rarely comes to you. You need to earn success.

As mentioned, very few people write down their goals? Yet it has been proven that by writing down your goals, committing to them, reviewing them regularly and sharing your success and challenges with someone else you can achieve great things, far more than you would if you just "winged it".

However, most people can write a plan, but there is much more to consider. So many people start with great enthusiasm when setting out their annual plan, but as time goes by the excitement begins to drop until eventually, we find ourselves going back to our old routine. Why is this?

One of the main reasons people stop following the process is that annual goals are too far in the future. People often start to fall behind in the daily and weekly activities but believe it is okay to do that as they can catch up later. That is the start of the slippy slope. However, there is a way around this issue, and that is to have goals that you can achieve in a shorter timeframe. One of the best methods is to set 100-day plans. The goals that you set in the 100-days are standalone, and while they may form part of your 12-month objectives, the result of achieving your goals will mean that you can celebrate your successes more often. One of the reasons this works is that you have more deadlines to meet and therefore you will focus far better than the more long-term annual plan.

If you want to avoid procrastination and achieve more than you ever thought possible then:

1. Visualise your Goal
2. Write down what you want to achieve.
3. Prioritise what you want to achieve.
4. Set your Objective for the year
5. Set your Goals for the next 100-days
    a. Breakdown your goals into tasks over 14 weeks (98 days)
    b. Review your weekly tasks each day
6. Commit to your goals.
7. Breakdown your weekly tasks into simple daily activities.
8. Start each day by reviewing your Weekly tasks by going through what you need to achieve that day.
9. End each day by recognising what you have achieved.
10. Work with somebody that will speak to you regularly about your progress.
11. Plan your time effectively.
12. When you find yourself procrastinating recognise what you are doing and why you are doing it. Then plan what you will do next time when you are in a similar situation.

The twelve steps fit into most situations and activities. If you want to learn a new language, then you need to plan how many words or phrases you will memorise each day which will build into your weekly target. Your weekly achievement will then reflect your 100-day goal. It would be best if you also planned what other tasks you would need to complete to be able to speak the language. That may include learning a memory technique, registering for a course or taking a holiday in the country. However, you get the idea there really is nothing to stop us but the fear we hold in ourselves.

Choosing your goals is something that you should take some time over. The goals should be important to your company, your team and yourself. That means aligning your personal goals, and your team goals with the goals of your company or organisation. You can get creative with this and look to see how your part of the organisation can overachieve.

Remember if you set goals that are too far into the future you will tend to procrastinate and delay the tasks, as you will feel you will be able to catch up with the tasks at a later date. Procrastination is what happens to most goals that are set so far into the future. By setting goals that are in the near future, you will find that you need to keep on top of the tasks you have set. The closer deadline pushes us to more significant activity. Start writing down all the critical goals that are urgent in each category, that is, your organisation's goals, your team goals and your goals. You will need to review each one and see where you can combine some of the goals. It is essential that you don't have too many goals. The number varies depending upon the amount of work that each goal demands. Leaders tend to work with no more than five goals at a time for both themselves and their team.

Now you have some planning to do. When will the goals need to be completed? Have you the resources to achieve the goals? Have you the skillsets in your team? What issues do you envisage that might hinder the progress towards the goal? It is amazing how writing your goals down and then documenting how you will achieve the goals helps in fixing a plan in your mind, when you have completed writing the list of goals you need to prioritise them.

SMART goals

Remember to make your goals SMART. SMART is an acronym and stands for Specific, Measurable, Achievable, Relevant and Time-Bound.

- Specific – Make your goal as specific as you can
- Measurable – if you cannot measure your goal how do you know if you are achieving it?
- Achievable – Having a goal of "Walking on the Moon" may be something that you would like to do. However, is it possible?
- Relevant – Is the goal pertinent to what you are trying to achieve in your business life?
- Time-Bound – without a time limit goals will inevitably drift into the future.

Here are three examples of SMART Goals:

1. In the next 100-days, we will increase the sales of our services by 20% above the same period last year.
    a. Specific – We will increase sales of our services
    b. Measurable – 20% above the same period last year
    c. Achievable – Assuming you have looked and seen you have the capacity
    d. Relevant – Relevant to your organisation's goals and targets
    e. Time-Bound – 100-days.
2. In the next 100-days, we will speak to each of our customers to ask what they think of our products and services
    a. Specific – We will talk to each of our Customers

   b. Measurable – In the next 100-days
   c. Achievable – Assuming you have the capacity
   d. Relevant – Relevant to the Business Customer Service Goals
   e. Time-Bound – 100-days
3. In the next 100-days, we will reduce the amount of paper we produce by at least 25%.
   a. Specific – Reduce the amount of paper we produce
   b. Measurable - By at least 25%. 25% will be successful any more will be a bonus
   c. Achievable – This may or may not be true.
   d. Relevant – Such a goal could reduce costs and therefore increase the profitability of the organisation.
   e. Time-Bound – 100-days

Now how are you going to set your goals for you and your team? The first thing to do is to have a clear idea of what you want to achieve, which can be project-based or be a business target. The main thing is that you have a clear understanding of your aims. The next thing is to split that objective into distinct parts, short, medium and long-term goals. In a sales environment that may well mean having 120% of the sales quota as the long-term annual objective. Now you can break the annual target into three 100-day periods. You have a choice of how you split the annual objective, for example, you can look to achieve 30% of the yearly goal by the end of the first period, 30% by the end of the second 100-days and 40% by the end of the third 100-day period. That would leave the final part of the year to overachieve your target and set up the following year. Naturally, the sales will not appear just because you have committed the numbers to a plan. The next step is to break down the objective into small tasks. These main tasks are allocated in your 100-day goals and are then broken down into 14 weeks, in each of which is the daily activities. How many calls should you make each day? How many meetings with prospects should you arrange each week? How many events should you attend in the 100 days?

Planning your day into small chunks of time can make a huge difference in how active you and your team are. As a leader, events will happen during the day that can disrupt your planned day, but there are methods which you can use to ensure you still get the essential things completed. One way is having "Red" and "Blue" times. If you have a red sign on your door or, in an open office environment, a red object on your desk you should not be disturbed unless it is critical. A blue sign on your door or a blue object on your desk will mean that you are available. Another method is to allocate time each day when you are available to meet members of your team. While this may take some time to get used to it works really well. The simple ideas are often the best.

Action Plan – Part 1

You now have three things that you want to do. Now it is time to plan how you get to your Goal.

When you write a Goal always add why you want to do it.

Eg. I will lose 5 kilograms in 100-days because I want to go on holiday looking great.

You will notice that this is where you need to be SMART

Be **S**pecific, make sure your task is **M**easurable, **A**chievable, **R**ealistic and is **T**ime-bound.

Goal 1
______________________________ ______________________________

Goal 2
______________________________ ______________________________

Goal 3
______________________________ ______________________________

As an example, if you want to "complete a project" that is very general so let's make it a SMART objective.

My team will complete the project in 100-days meeting the budget of £40,000.

Alternatively, If you want to "meet the sales targets" think of the following statement.

I will make x% of the sales target by (insert date).

Both Goals are Specific, Measurable, Achievable, Realistic, and Time-bound.

Once we have our 3 Goals, we need to break down the goals into Tasks. Don't worry about the size of the tasks as we will break the big ones down later.

Action Plan – Part 2

This exercise will get you starting to think about what you will need to do to achieve your Goal.

Goal 1
Task 1
Task 2
Task 3
Task 4
Task 5
Task 6
Task 7
Task 8
Task 9
Task 10

Goal 2
Task 1
Task 2
Task 3
Task 4
Task 5
Task 6
Task 7
Task 8
Task 9
Task 10

Goal 3

Task 1
Task 2
Task 3
Task 4
Task 5
Task 6
Task 7
Task 8
Task 9
Task 10

Action Plan - Part 3

Goal 1 – The objective for the next 14 weeks .
Week 1 - Date Goal 1 Task 1 – Goal 2 Task 1 – Goal 3 Task 1 –
Week 2 - Date Goal 1 Task 1 – Goal 2 Task 1 – Goal 3 Task 1 –
Week 3 - Date Goal 1 Task 1 – Goal 2 Task 1 – Goal 3 Task 1 –

Week 4 - Date Goal 1 Task 1 – Goal 2 Task 1 – Goal 3 Task 1 –

Week 5 - Date Goal 1 Task 1 – Goal 2 Task 1 – Goal 3 Task 1 –
Week 6 - Date Goal 1 Task 1 – Goal 2 Task 1 – Goal 3 Task 1 –
Week 7 - Date Goal 1 Task 1 –

Goal 2
Task 1 –

Goal 3
Task 1 –

Week 8 - Date
Goal 1
Task 1 –

Goal 2
Task 1 –

Goal 3
Task 1 –

Week 9 - Date
Goal 1
Task 1 –

Goal 2
Task 1 –

Goal 3
Task 1 –

Week 10 - Date
Goal 1
Task 1 –

Goal 2
Task 1 –

Goal 3 Task 1 –
Week 11 - Date Goal 1 Task 1 – Goal 2 Task 1 – Goal 3 Task 1 –
Week 12 - Date Goal 1 Task 1 – Goal 2 Task 1 – Goal 3 Task 1 –
Week 13 - Date Goal 1 Task 1 – Goal 2 Task 1 – Goal 3 Task 1 –
Week 14 - Date Goal 1 Task 1 –

Goal 2
Task 1 –

Goal 3
Task 1 –

Action Plan - Part 4

Now fill in this form each day. Have you completed a task or have you done something towards a task?

The spaces are deliberately small, so you need to be brief.

Week x of 14	Goal 1	Goal 2	Goal 3
Monday			
Tuesday			
Wednesday			
Thursday			
Friday			

Saturday			
Sunday			

Action Plan – Part 5

Most people use their online dairy such as Outlook to add tasks and then mark them as complete when the work is complete. However, you can use this paper method if you prefer.

No.	Description	Completed By

The things I have achieved this week towards my Goals are:

Commitment

Many people have started the process of setting their goals. Some people write their goals down and even go as far as breaking down the goals into tasks. However, they still don't achieve their goals. Why? The main reason is lack of commitment. Commitment is where we start to visualise how we will feel when we meet our goal. We close our eyes and envision hitting that target. We commit to all the hard work that will be needed and to the sacrifices that we will need to make. Helping your team in this visualisation technique will significantly improve their chances of being successful.

Commitment is the key to achieving goals. According to the Cambridge Dictionary, the definition of commitment is "a willingness to give your time and energy to something that you believe in, or a promise or firm decision to do something" An example of commitment is the company's commitment to Customer Service or your commitment to your goal. How committed will you or your team be? Do you mean that you will continuously review what you have done? Alternatively, do you expect you will give this a high priority and focus on the goal until it is complete? Will you do whatever it takes to achieve your goal?

Commitment is a verb. It is a doing word. Think of commitment as a pledge to yourself. However, there are varying degrees of commitment, and you and your team should understand where on the scale you are. If you are not fully committed people will find every opportunity to look for other things to do, they will become easily distracted and will discover goals will drift into the future. The goal is never completed. Does this sound familiar? That initial excitement diminished with time, and the goal becomes a burden. At this stage, you and your team need to look at what you meant when you said you were committed to the goal.

Review and Accountability

Once we have fully committed to our goal, we need to look at how we are going to manage the successes and setbacks as we move towards the goal. After setting up the goal, the tasks need to complete that goal and committing to the goal we need to be aware of where we are in relation to achieving the goal. The first thing to do is to write down what you have done at the end of each day in the Action Plan document or a diary, either a paper diary or an electronic diary. The next is to have a regular meeting with someone to discuss the progress and any issues you are finding. Having someone to review the progress of any goal will help you drive towards that goal.

Accountability is an essential step in helping you and your team achieve your goals. Taking responsibility for the goal, writing it down and having a process of assessing the progress will mean that you are far more likely to reach your target. Remember, goals are not met just because you have written them down; reviewing the goals is essential. Life happens, and deadlines are missed. The important thing is that you do not bury your head in the sand. Having a regular review of the goals is essential. A monthly review will give you and your team time to complete the majority of the tasks and understand where the target of some tasks was too optimistic.

In Chapter 3 Training, Coaching and Mentoring we discussed the GROW (Goal, current Reality, Options, and the Way forward). REGROW is where you Review and Evaluate the previous month's objectives before going through the same process of setting tasks and responsibilities. For teams, we use the GROUP (Goal, current Reality, Options, other people's Understanding, and the processes to Proceed) and then we would use the REGROUP method of reviewing tasks before assigning tasks and responsibilities. To ensure that each person is accountable for their goals use these methods at your regular meetings when you discuss your goals.

So, to avoid procrastination and achieve your goal, make sure you and your team commit to your goals, you and they have a clear focus, you help plan their tasks and set the completion of the tasks by an agreed time. Then work with individuals in the team to help them through the process. Will you and your team be one of the less than 1% to do this?

One final thing, when you or your team have achieved your goal remember to celebrate.

Chapter 5

Decision Making and Critical Thinking

Decision Making

There are many thoughts about "The Meaning of Life". What drives our decision making, what are we looking to achieve? Aristotle wrote, "Happiness is the meaning and purpose of life, the whole aim and end of human existence". Indeed the American Constitution states "We hold these truths to be self-evident, that all men are created equal, that they are endowed by their Creator with certain unalienable Rights, that among these are Life, Liberty and the pursuit of Happiness".

If we are seeking happiness in our decision making, what does that mean? Happiness is a state of mind where, what we say, what we do, and what we think are in harmony. Of course, that is only true when you are not having an adverse effect on the people around you. There is a point where the happiness of the masses outweighs the pleasure of the individual.

However, how does that affect our way of thinking and the decisions that we make every day? In general, most of us make decisions for the greater good. Decisions made in our business life are generally made to enhance and grow our company or organisation, our team and ourselves. As you will have discovered in the chapter 'Understanding Who You Are' we are all influenced by our experience. This chapter looks a little deeper at how we make decisions and how with a bit of extra thought we can give ourselves and the people we lead a better chance of success.

We all make decisions every day. Some of those decisions don't require too much thought, but some will have an impact on the future. Have you ever thought about why you come to a conclusion? What was it that helped you decide which way to go?

The human brain is fascinating and is capable of making complex calculations and decisions every second. We are continually bombarded with data and information from so many sources which demand our attention, and we are constantly asked to decide what is right or wrong, or which is the best or worst. People and organisations are desperate to catch your attention and promote their service or product. How can we make decisions with all that activity?

The answer is that we pass most of the mundane decision making to our subconscious. When we do this, the conscious part of the brain can focus on the matters which take up more thought. Asking someone what 9 x 9 is would most likely get the answer 81 without too much thought. However, asking someone a multiplication that is unlikely to be remembered such as, what is 19 x 17 the subconscious part of the brain would need to pass the calculation to the conscious mind. The conscious mind would then compute the answer, which is 323. That description may be a little clumsy, but you get the idea. The brain functions on autopilot until it comes across a problem that it cannot readily solve.

Therefore, when you face a scenario where you need to make a decision your subconscious brain looks for a previous decision you have made in similar circumstances. If there has been a similar circumstance, you will come to the same conclusion, without giving it too much conscious thought. When you realise this, it is a little disconcerting. How many choices have you made because you were in familiar territory? Were these the correct decisions? Did you assess all the possible outcomes? What was the result of your choice? Is there a different way to look at significant challenges and issues?

Critical Thinking

The way we make decisions and seeking different ways to look at problems we face has puzzled people for thousands of years; indeed the term "Critical Thinking" goes back to Socrates and his pupil Plato in ancient Greek times.

What about the mood you were in when you made the decision? Studies have shown that if you make a decision when you are angry, you are more likely to take risks. So, the next time a sales quota is missed, and you have an angry reaction, be careful as you are likely to up the ante and take a risk. Equally when you are happy you are more likely to see the positive side in any advice. So, when you want to get a favourable decision from someone you need to create a "happy" environment. Just be aware when someone is creating a "happy" environment for you.

Critical Thinking is looking at challenges and issues from a logical perspective. It is the ability to analyse the problem, theorise about the likely outcomes and come to a conclusion based on the facts. Basing your decision on facts seems very logical and the way most of us make decisions. However, is that true? When we make a decision, we generally base that decision on our previous experience and our own "belief system". Our belief system forms as we grow up and comes from our parents, family, friends, peers and community. We often follow beliefs without much forethought. The reason for this is due to the way our brain works.

Critical Thinking is the ability to look at each problem from a unique perspective which is often referred to as metacognition or meta-thinking which means 'thinking about thinking'. One of the critical skills is to have the ability to question your thinking. Why did I come to that conclusion? What previous experience have I had that has influenced me? Who has influenced my decision? What is the impact of drawing the opposite conclusion?

There are a few fundamental questions that you need to ask when you start to assess a situation. Some of those questions should be:

- Who has brought you the situation?
- What was their mood?
- What do you think of this person?
- When did they bring you the issue?
- Have you made a similar decision in similar circumstances before?
- Is the previous decision relevant?
- Would this make a difference to you or your company's goals?
- Why is it important to make a decision now?
- What is the impact of this decision?
- If there was no decision, what would be the impact?
- Have you got all the facts that would allow you to make a decision?
- Have you given yourself enough time to think about the situation?
- Have you a bias that would affect your conclusion?
- Who else should you involve in this situation?

Moreover, once you have made a decision ask yourself "Why have I come to this conclusion?

The purpose is to think about thinking.

There is a downside to Critical Thinking, and that is we could end up going around and around in circles. Analysing all the facts and trying to understand the likely consequences of any decision can lead to no decision at all. It is therefore advisable to use the

techniques of Critical Thinking but to have a time limit on when you intend to make a decision.

You may well be thinking that you usually follow the process. That is a natural thought, but that is using your subconscious mind. By bringing this process into your conscious mind, you will give yourself the opportunity to make a well balanced, well thought and impartial decision.

So, the next time you have an important decision to make why not give it a try?

Many models have been developed to explain how we come to decisions. One such model is The Chimp Paradox by Professor Steven Peters. In his book, he simplifies the brain into three components, the Human Mind, the Chimp Mind and the Computer. When we are developing in the womb, two brains form at the same time. One is logical, develops empathy and leans towards a social setting which is the Human Mind. The second brain functions on a lower level and is emotionally focused, the continuation of the species, territory management, whether to flee, fight or freeze and is (at times) illogical which is the Chimp Mind. Only after the two brains have been formed do they start to join together with connections. Either of these two brains can run your decision making. However, a third brain the Computer is built. The third brain is the "hard disc" which records our experiences. It is where both the Human and Chimp brains input experiences and then refer to when they have a decision to make. All three brains have the capability of running your life. When all brains agree there is no issue. However, when there is a dispute a problem arises. How you can distinguish between the Human and the Chimp minds and how you manage the Chimp mind are the major topics of the book.

If you are to lead a team, you should have an understanding of how you come to decisions. It doesn't matter what model you use to

gain an understanding of your thought process as long as you understand how you make decisions.

Here are three exercises that you can use to understand what dominates your decision making.

Exercise 1 – Decision Making

1. List all the important decisions that you have made during the last week.

2. Start a diary and list all the choices that you make each day. You will be amazed when you compare both lists. You will find that you make far more choices than you believe.

3. Mark all the decisions that were new situations.

4. As you make your decision, make two lists one where the decisions were without too much thought. The second list will be where you spent some time assessing all the facts.

Now, look at the decisions that will have an impact on you, your teams' or your company's goals or success. How many of those decisions did you make without too much thought? These are the decisions that you need to be aware of and ensure you are focusing on all the facts.

Review each of these decisions and ask yourself if you made the correct decision. If you did not make the right decisions, then look at how you might review the situation. Sometimes it is not possible to reverse a course of action if that is the case you will need to continue on the path you have set. However, at least you are now aware of the likely impact. You will also start to understand how you can change the decision the next time something similar arises.

Exercise 2 – How your mood affects your decision making

The decisions we make are influenced by how we feel at the time. The next activity is to look at the list you created in Exercise 1 and think about what mood you were in when you made the decision.

1. Put a "+" sign by all the decisions you made when you were happy
2. Put a "-" sign by all the decisions you made when you were not happy

Now you have a list look at it and ask the question, why?

You may well be surprised at the answer to those questions. Remember, you will make confident decisions when you are happy, and you will take higher risks when you are angry. Often the things that make us feel unhappy or angry are related to past experiences. Those experiences may well have happened some time ago and will now be irrelevant. However, you still feel unhappy or angry.

Making decisions based on your mood is your belief system at work. The good news is that you can change your belief system. By understanding what made you unhappy, you can start to retrain your thoughts. Focus on the event that triggered your feeling. Some people describe the feeling like one of unease; you feel uncomfortable and will not be looking forward to the situation. Usually, writing a report is mentioned and when people start to analyse why they discover that a document they have completed in the past had a lot of negative comments or the report took a lot of time and effort, and you feel the paper was not valued by your colleagues. While that document may well have been less than perfect, it does not mean all documents you write will have with the same comments or have the same outcome. However, our mind only understands that we are writing a report and then relays the same feelings you had when you published the original document. If you know that process, you can start to look at the process more logically. Since you wrote the report that was poorly received you have gained a lot more experience, you have written

many more reports that had a more favourable outcome; it is not logical to feel unhappy about something that you have yet to complete.

All this will start to help you feel more positively about your new project. You will find that you begin to feel more optimistic and because of that, the document you are writing will start to flow far easier. You will still need to review your report and check it for accuracy and grammar, but that feeling you had when you started will no longer hold you back.

If you practice Critical Thinking each day, you will start to become aware of why you are making decisions. The aim of assessing the crucial choices we make every day is not to change the outcome of those decisions but to be aware of why we made those decisions so that we can justify them.

Chapter 6

The Art of Effective Speaking

Have you ever thought of how you communicate with the people around you? Most people believe that communication is mainly in the form of speaking or writing. However, communication is far more than talking and writing. You are always communicating with people around you. Nonverbal communication, which is detailed in Chapter 7 Body Language, accounts for around 60% of what people receive from you. So, before you start to speak people have already formed an opinion of you.

The dictionary has some definitions of communication. They include:

- The imparting or exchanging of information by speaking, writing or using some other medium.
- A letter or message containing information or news.
- The successful conveying or sharing of ideas and feelings.

More definitions of communication relate to technology. However, all of these definitions rely on two things. The first is that the provider of information is clear and precise; the second is that the receiver of the information interprets the data and has the same understanding as the giver of the data. If one of these pieces is missing, then there is a strong chance of miscommunication. Therefore, we need to be very careful of both what we communicate and how we relate.

The good news is that we are very good at interpreting the information that we receive. We do this by using the subconscious part of our brain. As we are collecting data, we process it and compare it against our experience and come to a conclusion. Understanding this process can help us become a great communicator and leader. As an example, have you thought about how you greet people when you first meet them? Do you smile (nonverbal), offer your hand for a handshake (nonverbal), walk towards them (nonverbal) and say, "Hello, how are you"? As you can see the person you are meeting will have an opinion of you before you speak.

In this chapter, we will focus on what you say and how you say it.

Speaking

Speaking is the first thing that we usually think about when we discuss communication. The words we use and how we use them is crucial. The development of our vocabulary comes in our early years when our parents, siblings and our extended family had a significant influence as we go through life our work, role, education and local community influence how we speak and the words that we use. If we talk, we are therefore not only communicating the words we are also expressing where we are from, our level of education, the type of organisation we work for and our role within that organisation. As we speak, we are communicating far more than we think we are.

Speaking is not just about the words we are using. The person we are speaking to interprets what is being said by a combination of things such as body language, posture, facial expression, the pace of the delivery and the tone of voice.

When you are speaking to an individual or a group of people there are some things that you should do if you want to be a good communicator:

- Talk slowly. Typically, good talkers don't rush into a conversation. By talking slowly, you will give your audience more time to understand what you are saying and time to formulate questions that will provide them with a far better understanding of what you are trying to communicate.
- Be aware of your tone. Are you speaking with a "teacher-child" tone? Are you speaking with a sarcastic tone? We often don't realise how we are being heard. So, practice listening to your tone.
- Be aware of the volume of your voice. Are you speaking too softly, or too loudly? If people are straining to hear your voice, they will not be able to concentrate on your message. Equally, if you are speaking too loudly, people will assume you are rude or disrespectful; either way, your message is not being heard.
- Hold eye contact. When people talk, they tend to hold eye contact for less time than when they are listening. Therefore, people notice if you are not keeping eye contact and see this as either avoiding them or that you are hiding something. So, when speaking to an individual or small group, it is vital to have eye contact as this communicates that you are interested in them as well as the subject you are discussing.
- There is nothing worse than speaking to someone when they appear to be reading from a script. Speaking without showing any emotion leads people to view the discussion as boring. If we are passionate about a subject, we will naturally express our feelings.
- Anecdotes are a great way of reinforcing your point. Offering insights into a subject will demonstrate your understanding.

- Know your audience and use the best words. It seems obvious, but the best words to use will depend on the topic of conversation and the people you are addressing. Addressing a group of students with complicated acronyms from your industry might well demonstrate your knowledge, but it is unlikely that they will see you as a good speaker. However, on the other hand, using simple language to a group of experienced and skilled colleagues will not go down well either.
- When people react to what you are saying, either verbally or nonverbally make a mental note or, where appropriate, ask if they would like to contribute to the conversation. By reacting to someone's comments or questions, you are demonstrating that their opinion is valued which will enhance your reputation as a good speaker.

There are some different situations when we are speaking; they include formal and informal meetings, one on one discussions, talking to a large group, speaking on the telephone, and public speaking. Each of these situations requires different skills. There are times when we move naturally from one type of talking to another, but we should think about how our message is heard and understood in each of these situations and adjust where necessary. One common attribute for all these situations is the ability to listen and adapt your speech to reflect what you have heard.

- One on one discussions. Speaking to a person is something we do every day, many times. We tend to do this on autopilot. The next time you are having a conversation become aware of the other person's body language, really listen to what they are saying and when you are speaking be mindful of your pace, volume, and tone which might sound a lot for you to do, but with practice, it will become second nature.

- Formal meetings. It would be best if you always prepared for a formal meeting. Knowing the subjects that you are to discuss and preparing adequately will demonstrate your speaking prowess. Speaking confidently about a topic is vital if you want to be seen as a good speaker.
- Informal meetings. Speaking at a casual event gives you an excellent opportunity to express yourself. Be self-aware of what you are saying and know who is listening to you. Be aware of the nonverbal responses to your points and check to see if everybody understands. However, don't be overpowering, don't let your enthusiasm get carried away.
- Speaking to a large group. Talking to a large group of people is different from presenting to a large group of people, this is where you have some information that you want to communicate, but there are no slides or props. The audience focuses on you. Remember that around 60% of communication is nonverbal and you will set the tone for your speech before you start speaking. To establish a positive mood, you should stand up straight, look confident, smile, and look your audience in the eye. Pick a few people out and smile at them. Take a deep breath and start speaking, slowly.
- Speaking on the phone. When talking on the phone the pace, volume and tone of your speech are vital. Because your body language cannot be assessed the person at the other end of the phone can only judge your message through your voice and this often leads to miscommunication. A skilled speaker will ensure that the listener understands the message by asking them to summarise the content of the conversation.

- Speaking over the internet. Having discussions over the internet is becoming more common. When we use systems with no visual capability, the skills we use when talking on the telephone are similar to those we use when speaking on the internet. There are times when we are speaking to many people on the internet such as when we host a webinar. When you are talking to many people, you should always check if your message is being heard and keep asking your audience questions that relate to the points that you are presenting. Most webinars use some presentation technique which gives your audience an idea of the points you are making. However, don't make your slides too busy and whatever you do don't read from the slides as this will turn your audience off. The use of the chat facility to check if your audience understands your message is an excellent way of verifying that your message is heard.
- Public Speaking. Many books and videos on the internet offer help when you are being asked to speak at an event. There are a few techniques and offers of advice that are common to most of the articles. They include:
    - It is natural to be nervous
    - Know your subject
    - Know your audience
    - Before you start, remember to take a few deep breaths
    - Don't speak too quickly
    - Pauses are very powerful
    - Reading from slides puts an audience off
    - Anecdotes, where relevant, are compelling
    - If you want people to hear critical points in your message, you will need to repeat it at least six times.

- Tell them what you are going to tell them, tell them, and then tell them what you have told them.
- Know where you will be presenting
- Know the tools you will be expected to use
- Know your timings
- Practise
- Use props in proportion to your speech

As with all forms of speaking the pace of your delivery, the volume and the tone are very important and so is the way you stand, the expression on your face, the way you look at the audience, and the way you use hand gestures are all just as important.

It is also imperative to understand how you or those that you are communicating with can put up barriers when you are speaking. There are some natural barriers that we all use. Sometimes these methods are excellent especially when you want to move to close the conversation; however, most will only stop the person you are speaking with from communicating openly. The more you understand these barriers, the more you can use them to understand the person and/or the audience.

Communication Blockers

Here are 7 Communication Blockers:

1. Interrupting shows, you aren't interested in what someone is saying. The person you are speaking to will stop expressing their views which is fine if you want to ensure your position is understood but not if you're interested in the other persons' point of view.

2. "Why" questions. They tend to make people defensive. By asking "why" you are asking the other person to justify their point of view. The question "why" can be used very effectively if you use it to clarify a point, however, only if you acknowledge what was said and then ask the person speaking to continue, but constantly asking "why" will quickly bring a conversation to a halt.

3. Quick reassurance, saying things like, "Don't worry about that." Such statements can be very dismissive; you haven't acknowledged that the speaker has a valid point.

4. Advising "I think the best thing for you is to ...." Your advice may well be valid but before offering it always ask what the speaker would suggest. A better way to advise is to say, "Would you consider......?"

5. Digging for information and forcing someone to talk about something they would rather not discuss. Look out for the other person's body language. If they start to look away or to fidget, then you should understand that they are uncomfortable about the subject. There are times when you should try to probe further. However, you should always ask their permission to do that. A great way of doing that is to say, "I am getting the impression that this is making you feel uncomfortable, do you mind if we explore that subject a little deeper"? Always respect the answer if the answer is no, stop. There will be other occasions when you can broach the subject again.

6. Patronising "You poor thing, I know just how you feel." People don't react well when they feel people are looking down on them.

7. Preaching "You should. . ." Alternatively, "You shouldn't. . ." During a discussion, people are not always looking for a

solution. Often, they want to ensure that their point is heard. Before you start to offer advice, you should make sure you understand and agree on the points. It is never a good idea to tell people what they should or shouldn't do. A better approach would be to ask them what solution they would suggest. If there is no obvious answer, a good response would be "Have you considered .....?

Speaking Objective

When you are speaking, you should be aware of what you are trying to achieve. Are you trying to impart information, or are you trying to entertain? What do you want your audience to do once you have finished speaking?

If you aim to impart information, have you prepared a way for your audience to demonstrate that they have listened and understood the subject matter? If it is a one on one discussion, it is relatively easy to ask questions that will confirm that your points are appreciated. It is a little more difficult if you are speaking to a small group of people but asking pertinent questions at the end of the talk should help demonstrate that your audience has gained some knowledge on the subject. The most challenging situation is where you are speaking to a broader audience which is where the best way to gauge their understanding is to ask for questions at the end of your speech. If the room is silent it means one of two things, either you were so good that everybody understood what you were saying and there is no need for further clarification, or your message has fallen on deaf ears. Either way, the best way out of a quiet room is to have a few questions prepared that emphasise your key points.

If you want people to see you as a leader, you will need to be able to speak effectively in all situations, some people are natural speakers, but they are few and far between. The best way to become a good speaker is to practice. Look for opportunities that will allow you to speak to a small group of people. After any speech ask for feedback, and if there are any negative comments don't take them personally. Accept them as constructive criticism that will help you get better at the craft of effective speaking.

Chapter 7

Body Language

One common trait among leaders is that they seem to have an intuition of when things are going well and when things are going wrong. You will find that leaders are ahead of the issues that concern you. However, you hadn't mentioned those issues to anyone. Leaders are very good at picking up nonverbal signals and then reacting on them. They are very good at reading Body Language.

There have been many books and online articles about Body Language and how it can help you determine what someone is thinking. As discussed in Chapter 6 The Art of Effective Speaking the words we speak along with the tone, inflexion and volume make up only 40% of communication. That leaves 60% for nonverbal communication.

Body Language or nonverbal communication is something we do all the time, without thought. It is where the brain reacts to the world reflectively and instantaneously, and in real time.

Body Language accounts for such a significant part of communication, and so it is imperative to understand what message you are conveying with your body. Body Language is how you express yourself with your eyes, facial expressions, arm movement, body position, and leg position. The critical thing about Body Language is that it is tough to fool people. Body Language is natural and while the body can give off a series of false messages for a short time, it will revert to the true nature and feelings after a while. You should be aware that Body Language should be taken as a whole; seeing someone who is scratching their ear may reflect that they are hiding something, but it can also mean that their ear is itching. However, seeing someone that is fidgeting, scratching their ear and is avoiding eye contact would strongly suggest that they are hiding something.

Lying, to some degree, is something that we do all the time. You may not agree with that but stop to think for a moment. What if everybody told the absolute truth to everybody all the time. When asked what you think about a piece of work, do you say 'It's okay, I particularly like the way you have approached the task? Can you explain your conclusion as I am not sure how you got there?' Alternatively, do you say ' That is not what I asked you for, it is the worst piece of work I have seen for a long time, and by the way, please come in a clean shirt tomorrow'? Which one would encourage a better piece of work the next time? Which would help build morale? The point is that we often tone down what we are thinking to keep control of situations

Eyes

The way our eyes react and respond when we are communicating is generally out of our conscious control. By studying peoples eye contact and movement, you will gain a good understanding of what they are thinking.

They say that eyes are the window to our soul. The eyes give us a great insight (pardon the pun) into what people are thinking. We all use expressions such as 'look me in the eye when you say that', 'she has piercing eyes', 'his eyes are so deep', 'he looked daggers at him', 'she looked right through me'. We also say a person is hard, angry, blank, sad, happy, defiant, cold, jealous, and unforgiving. What we are observing is the dilation of the other person's pupils which is something that we cannot consciously control and so gives a real indication of what the other person is thinking or feeling.

When two people are speaking, they will subconsciously look at each other in the eye and form an opinion. When our eyes start to dilate it shows we are interested in what we are seeing. The reaction of the eyes makes the person we are talking to seem more attractive, and if we are similarly interested, then our pupils will start to dilate. That is why babies widen their eyes when you look at them; they understand that they will get more attention when they do that. It is also why children's best-selling toys have oversized pupils.

When observing a group of people, it is important to note that men and women have different types of vision. Experiments have shown that men have a tunnel vision and tend to focus on what is in front of them. Men have evolved tunnel vision because they needed to focus on the prey or threat ahead of them. Women, on the other hand, have a far better peripheral vision which means that they can gaze at a person without them realising it.

Generally speaking, the longer the eye contact between two people the more significant the interest. However, if we maintain eye contact too long the effect is precisely the opposite, and we are made to feel very uncomfortable. Michael Argyle, a pioneer of social psychology and nonverbal communication skills, found that when Westerners and Europeans talk, their average gaze time is 61 %, consisting of 41% gaze time when speaking, 75% when listening and 31% mutual gazing. He recorded the average gaze length to be 2.95 seconds, and the period of a mutual gaze was 1.18 seconds.

When we are listening, we spend up to 80% of the time maintaining eye contact. Michael Argyle showed that in most cultures you should keep eye contact around 60% to 70% of the time to gain a good rapport. If, however, you meet a timid person who is nervous and does not maintain eye contact, you will more than likely find this person untrustworthy. If you are in any negotiation you should, therefore, pay attention to your eye contact.

A person's eye movements can reveal what their mind is focusing on by telling you whether they remember something they have seen, heard, smelt, tasted or touched. This technique is a development of American psychologists Grinder and Bandler and is known as Neuro-linguistic Programming or NLP.

In simple terms, if a person remembers something that they saw, their eyes will move upward. If they recall something they heard, they look to the side and tilt their head as if listening. If they remember a feeling or emotion, they'll look down and to the right. When a person is mentally talking to themselves, they look down and to the left.

There are several gazes we use every day and in a book by Allan and Barbara Pease called Body Language the Definitive Book they give three examples:

The Social Gaze
This gaze is the one we use most often and centres in an inverted triangle between the eyes and the mouth. We spend up to 90% of gaze time doing this when we are communicating one on one. This gaze is a none aggressive gaze.

The Intimate Gaze

The Intimate Gaze is when we are approaching people the gaze centres between the eyes, and then we move our gaze below the chin. At close quarters we look to the chest to check the sex of the person we are meeting and from a distance we see further down. We are observing both the sex and the appearance of the person we are meeting. Then, we will then have a second gaze to ensure we have come to the correct conclusion. We then look at the persons face, all this an unconscious process and one that everybody does.

The Power Gaze

The Power Gaze is when we are in a serious conversation. The Power Gaze focuses between the eyes. You will notice that when people are using the Power Gaze, they don't blink as often as usual and maintain the gaze for longer than they usually would. The lack of blinking and the more extended stare makes the person they are speaking to feel uncomfortable. Which means you should be very careful with this gaze as it can stop conversations dead in its track.

There are other signals that the eyes give, such as blinking. Frequently people blink six to eight times per minute. When someone you are speaking to starts to blink more often than usual it indicates, they are not interested in what you are saying. It is as if their brain is trying to block you out. If they combine this with tilting their head-back, they are showing that they feel superior to you. In this case, whatever you are saying is not being heard, and so you need to try a different approach or move on.

If the person you are speaking to starts to move their eyes rapidly from side to side for a second or two, they are looking for an escape route which is a natural thing to do if you are feeling threatened or what you are hearing is of no interest.

Facial Expressions

Smiling is something we do every day but have you stopped to consider why you smile. It is a way of saying 'Look at me I am not a threat'. When we are born we quickly learn that crying gets peoples' attention and smiling ensures that they stay with us. Smiling is something we do naturally and without conscious thought. When we laugh, we use the muscles at the side of our face to pull the corners of our mouths up, and at the same time, we use the muscles around our eyes to squint which produces the crows-feet lines. You will notice that when someone is giving a false smile, they will bunch their cheeks and pull the corners of their mouths, but the muscles around the eyes will stay still. You can be sure when this happens that they are not amused.

There are five common types of a smile; they are:

- The Tight-Lipped Smile

  The Tight-Lipped Smile is used when we are hiding something. While we are smiling, we are not agreeing with what is being said. It is a sign of rejection.

- The Twisted Smile

The Twisted Smile is when one side of your mouth is smiling, and the other is frowning, another name for this smile is the sarcastic smile.

- The Bottom Jaw Smile

  When you drop your bottom jaw to reveal your teeth, bunch up your cheeks and squint your eyes. Bottom Jaw Smile is used to give the impression is laughing and playful.

- The Coy Smile

  The Coy Smile is when you smile by bunching your cheeks, pull the corners of your mouth up, squint your eyes, and lower your chin as if to protect your throat. The Cot Smile is a submissive smile and one that evokes the feeling of wanting to protect the person who is smiling.

- The Permanent Smirk

  Some people seem to have a permanent smile on their face. The Permanent Smile is used by politicians to show that they are in control and that everything is going well.

What is remarkable is that it has been found that people will reflect the face of the person that they are seeing and so smiling will have the effect of "making" people smile back. The subconscious reaction has the effect of people seeing you in a more positive light, and they are more likely to agree with you.

So, remember to keep smiling, even if that is not the way you are thinking.

Laughing

With smiling comes the sound of laughing. Smiling and laughing effects the brain.
They cause the brain to release endorphins which are a chemical that makes us feel happy. The harder we laugh; the more endorphins are released. That is one of the reasons why people turn to alcohol and drugs as they also release endorphins that make

you feel better. Of course, there is a downside because the more alcohol you consume, the more the effect on the Central Nervous System which results in feeling depressed. From a drugs perspective the "high" associated with taking the drugs is something that the user will continue to chase, but to reach the same level of euphoria more drugs will be needed. So laughing would appear to be the best medicine.

The act of smiling and laughing has a positive effect on your health as the endorphins that are released help the body's immune system and reduce stress. So, if you are feeling down look up a couple of movies that make you laugh and sit down to watch them. In a work environment try memorising a few jokes to tell your colleagues or send a few funny pictures that will put a smile on people's faces. If you are preparing a team event, try to include something that will help people see the funny side.

Arms and Hands

Did you know that there are more connections between the brain and the hands than any other part of our body? Therefore, we tend to use our hands a lot when we are communicating. How often have you heard the expression 'She speaks with her hands'? As with a lot of body language, most of what we do is at the subconscious level, and so it gives a fair indication of what we mean or what we are saying.

Open Palm

The palm is where we show if we are open and honest if we have something to hide, or we are feeling aggressive. We show the palm of our hand in the open position when we are demonstrating that we are telling the truth and want to emphasise that we have nothing to hide. When we are hiding something, we show the back of our hands or have the palms of our hands facing the floor which also demonstrates a feeling of power.

Closed Palm

If we are feeling aggressive, we sometimes clench our hands and use the index finger to point which is given even more emphasis when we use it to beat a time of whatever we are saying. It is like using an implement to 'beat your message'.

Pointing finger

So, if you are a finger pointer practice speaking with your palms open and this will have the effect of people seeing you as more accessible and, experiments have shown, will remember more of what you have said.

Another way of using your hands is to use the okay sign where your index and thumb touch which gives the appearance of someone who has authority but is none threatening.

Okay sign

For centuries handshaking has been used as a form of greeting. Initially, it was used to show that neither party had a weapon concealed about their person. In Roman times the wrist handshake was used as it was common practice to have a dagger hidden in your sleeve. By holding and shaking each other's wrist, you were checking to see if they had a concealed weapon.

The handshake as we understand it, where we clasp the palms of our hands together, started to be used in the 19th century where two people of equal standing would meet to conclude a deal.

Did you know that there are different types of handshakes? The main three are the dominant handshake, the submissive handshake and the equality handshake.

The dominant handshake is used by people who feel they have higher power than you, or they are trying to dominate you which is where the person who is offering the handshake holds his palm to the floor. The result is that you offer your hand in the submissive sign with your palm facing up. When you are offered the palm of their hand vertically, you shake in an equal position which gives rise to the saying, 'He has the upper hand'.

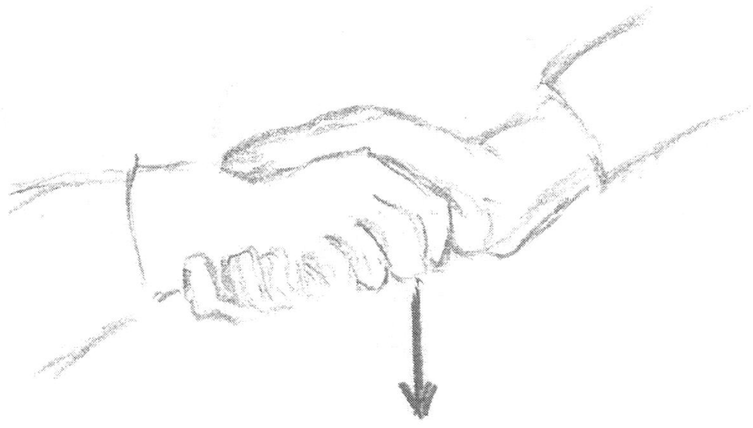

Dominant Handshake position is the one on the left.

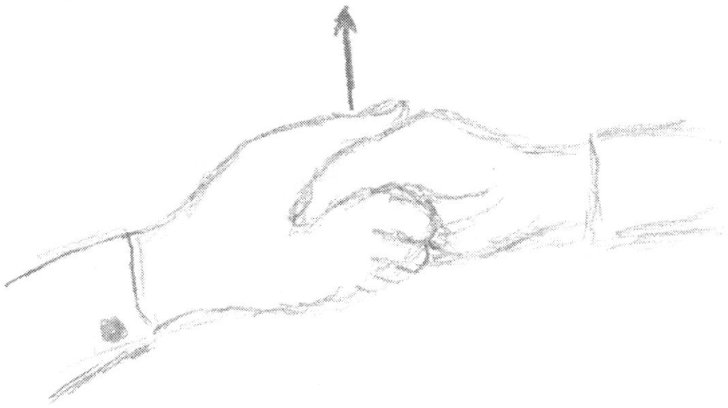

Submissive handshake position is the one on the left

There are ways of showing that you do not feel the person you are shaking hands with you is dominant. One way is to step across with your left leg so that they need to alter their body position; this gives you the opportunity to straighten the handshake. Another way is to place your left hand on top of the other persons' right hand which shows that you feel you are equal.

Some handshakes have an adverse effect on the people who are on the receiving end. The main two are the bone crusher, where the person squeezes your hand so hard it is painful which is usually done by someone who is trying to demonstrate that they are more powerful than you, or they feel insecure. The other type of handshake is the wet fish which is where the hand is feeble and sometimes clammy. We generally see this type of handshake as that of a vulnerable person; however, it may be because they have a profession where they use their hand and are trying to protect it.

The perfect handshake is the equal one, where you both offer the same pressure. If you feel the other person is using less force than you then relax your hand a little if you think the other person is using more force than you increase your pressure to match theirs. Using this technique will ensure that you are perceived as someone that is trustworthy.

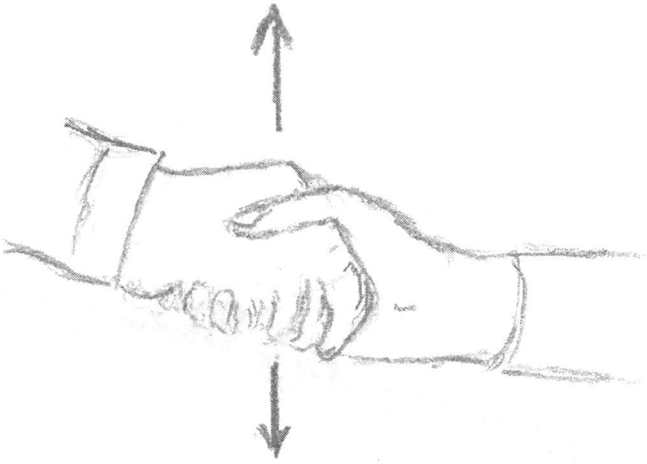

Equal Handshake

Arms

The way we use our arms when we are communicating goes back to our childhood. When we found something that we didn't like, or it was threatening we used to hide behind solid objects like tables and chairs, or adults when they were around. Later, we adapted this to folded arms. Folding our arms is defensive and is showing that we feel insecure or threatened. There are a few ways we try to disguise the fact that we are feeling anxious. One way is only to use one arm so that the hand reaches across the chest to hold the elbow of the other arm. Men will often play with their shirt cuff or cufflinks. There is a way to cross your arms but show you are in control, that is when you fold your arms and have your thumbs pointed up. Such a posture suggests you are in the presence of someone you feel is superior, but you also think that you have something to offer and may challenge that person's point of view.

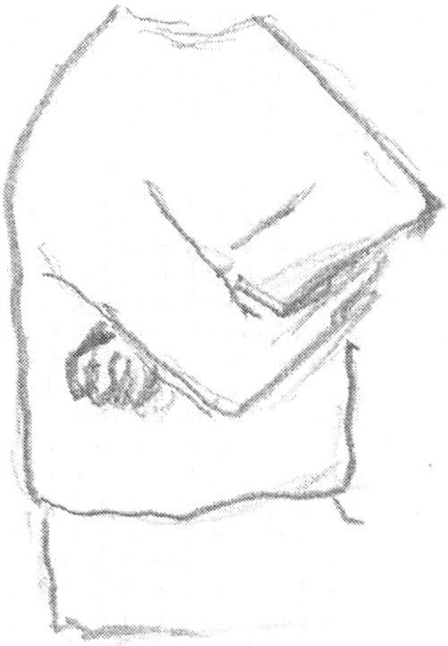

Not Sure

Closed opinion

In Control

Signals

Body Language can tell us a lot about what we are thinking especially if we are not telling the entire truth or if we feel somebody, we are speaking to is not being honest. When we are children, we automatically cover our eyes when we see something we don't like, we will also cover our ears when we don't want to hear something. So, it should be no surprise that we attempt to cover our mouths when we are saying something that we know is wrong.

As we grow the signals that we gave out as a child become more refined, but we still use the same signs. However, we are not aware that we are giving off those signs. If we are not telling the entire truth, we will brush our nose, or touch part of our mouth. If we are listening to someone and we believe that they are dishonest, we will use the same signal. If we are in a presentation and we don't believe something in the presentation, we will close our eyes or rub them gently. If we hear something we do not agree with, we will touch our ear or rub the side of our head. The question is, can we suppress our body language and fool the people with whom we are communicating? Such signals are deeply ingrained in our subconscious, and we cannot just switch them off. If we suppress the scratch to the nose, then we will give other signals such as rubbing the side of our cheeks, or we will become fidgety on our chair as we fight to stop our natural reaction.

If you want to know what somebody is thinking when you are negotiating with them, offer them a cup of coffee and watch where they place their cup. If the cup is in a position where they must cross their body to hold the cup they are feeling negative. However, If they place the cup so that their body is open when they reach for the cup, they like what you are saying, or what you are offering.

A way of influencing the person you are speaking to is to touch them lightly on the hand or the elbow, for no more than three seconds. Elbow and hand touching, when done discreetly, grabs attention, reinforces a comment, underlines a concept, increases your influence over others, makes you more memorable and creates positive impressions on everyone.

The next time you are at a meeting or a presentation make a mental note to observe how people react to something you are saying. You may be surprised at the result. The critical thing to remember is not to judge people when you notice something that you perceive as negative. Use it as an indication that your message is not being heard which will give you the opportunity to try a different approach or move on and look for another time to approach the subject again.

Chapter 8

The Art of Listening and Questioning

To be a leader of people does not mean that you should expect people to do everything that you instruct them to do. One of the main differences between managing and leading people is how you listen to the team, how you respond to their questions and how you question their assertions and assumptions.

Listening is a critical attribute that all leaders possess. Listening is a skill that we should all practice. Many people hear what is said, but they have not listened. They are too focused on their agenda. There is a big difference between hearing and listening. To hear someone means that you use your ear and acknowledge that someone is speaking. To listen to someone means that you are paying attention to what the speaker is saying. So, are you focused on the speaker's point of view or are you preparing your response before they have finished speaking?

Listening requires your full attention as most of what we are communicating is nonverbal. As described in Chapter 7 Body Language when someone is sceptical about a point, they may well raise their eyebrows when they agree with a point, and start to smile, conversely when someone disagrees with something that is being said you may well see a scowl. We all have many nonverbal ways of letting the speaker know how we feel. Body language is critical and the more you appreciate how it works, the more you will understand the speaker. However, putting too much emphasis on body language may mean that you miss the main points that the speaker is making.

Active Listening

Active Listening is the ability to focus entirely on what the speaker is saying, respond to what the speaker is saying and then to remember what was said. That may sound familiar, and most people will say that it how they listen. However, is it? Most people start to formulate a response to a speaker before they have finished speaking. Is that focusing on what the speaker is saying or is the listener concentrating on their own opinion of the subject? To listen properly, you should reserve your judgement on the subject under discussion and listen. Once you have heard what the speaker has said you should then summarise what you have heard and seek further clarification of the speaker's point. Only when you have clarified that you and the speaker have the same understanding of what was said should you prepare a response.

Always remember, when Active Listening the first thing you should do is to clear your mind of any preconceptions of the subject you are discussing. Remember what you are trying to do is to understand what the speaker is saying. The point is to focus on the topic of the discussion, are there some points that the speaker repeats that may mean that this is very important to them. Why is it important? Are they speaking quietly or are they animated, what is driving their emotion? If both parties agree, then it is time to dig a little deeper into the subject. Like an onion a topic has many layers, the first thing the speaker says is just the first layer, a skilled listener will pick up a few phrases or points that were raised and ask the speaker to explain them in greater detail.

There are sixteen skills listed below which will help people be better active listeners some of these skills you will undertake naturally, but some you won't. You do not have to become adept at each of these skills to be a good active listener; but the more you do, the better you'll be. The more you use these skills, the more you will find yourself listening to what the other person is saying to you.

1. Face the speaker
   Facing the speaker is essential, that way neither you or the speaker can get distracted

2. Maintain eye contact
   That doesn't mean staring at the speaker, but having eye contact will show that you are interested in the speaker and the subject that they are discussing

3. Listen without judgement
   Before you start a conversation recognise that you have preconceptions on the subject and put them to one side.

4. Give the person you are speaking to time to finish their point of view
   By giving people time while you are actively listening you are demonstrating that you are giving full attention to the subject.

5. Don't jump in.
   Don't rush to a conclusion. You may very well have a valid point, but by letting the other person finish, they may well cover the subject or issue that you were going to raise

6. Minimal encourager
   Use brief, positive prompts to keep the conversation going and show you are listening, e.g., "umm-hmmm," "Oh?" "I understand," "Then?" "And?"

7. Summarise
   When they have finished their point to show you are listening repeat what you think the other person said, not by parroting, but by paraphrasing what you heard in your own words. For example, "Let's see if I'm clear about this. ."

8. Giving feedback
   Let the person know what your initial thoughts are on the situation. Share pertinent information, observations, insights, and experiences. Then listen carefully to confirm.

9. Emotion labelling
   When responding or giving feedback try putting feelings into words as this will often help a person to see things more objectively. To support the person begin, use "door openers" for example, "I'm sensing that you're feeling frustrated, or worried, or anxious, or concerned."

10. Probing
    Ask questions to draw the person out and get deeper and more meaningful information for example, "What do you think would happen if you... .?", "have you considered...?"

11. Validation
    Acknowledge the individual's problems, issues, and feelings. Listen openly and with empathy, and respond interestingly for example, "I appreciate your willingness to talk about such a difficult issue. . ."

12. Effective pause

Deliberately pause at crucial points for emphasis. Pausing will tell the person you are saying something extremely important to them.

13. Silence
    Allow for comfortable silences to slow down the exchange. Give a person time to think as well as talk. Silence can also be very helpful in diffusing an unproductive interaction.

14. “I” messages
    By using "I" in your statements, you focus on the problem, not the person. An I-message lets the person know what you feel and why for example, "I know you are passionate about this, but I need to. . ."

15. Redirecting
    If someone is showing signs of being overly aggressive, agitated, or angry, this may be the time to shift the discussion to another topic or sub-topic. Redirecting the problem will reduce tension. However, it is also valid for you to ask why the speaker is showing the feelings you are observing. As a leader, it is up to your judgement when to redirect and when to dig further into the topic of conversation. If you do redirect the subject, you should make a point to revisit it at a later date when the tension is reduced.

16. Consequences
    Part of the feedback may involve talking about the possible effects of inaction. Take your cues from what the person is saying for example, “What happened the last time you ….?”

Become A Better Listener: Active Listening - Psych Central, https://psychcentral.com/lib/become-a-better-listener-active-listening/ (accessed March 31, 2019).

Leaders need to make informed decisions on many topics, and so the ability to listen to different points of view is vital. Those leaders that clearly understand the issues and are willing to discuss people's concerns by listening and, as importantly, understanding their point of view will be shown respect and will build a natural following.

Active listening and powerful questions come hand-in-hand, only by listening can you formulate the appropriate question.

Questioning

If we are to communicate effectively, then we must be able to ask powerful questions. Why powerful questions, and what are the powerful questions? Powerful questions are those that help us get a deeper understanding of the subject. They go beyond the obvious and will challenge assumptions and peoples bias, whether that is in the conscious or subconscious mind.

We all ask questions every day, but those questions tend to demonstrate that we already know the answer, or we try to direct the conversation towards our values, beliefs or bias. What tends to happen is that as someone is describing a subject, we formulate an opinion and then come up with a question. When the speaker has stopped speaking or paused for a breath, we leap in with our question, or we merely state that we understand what is said. The outcome is that the speaker and the receiver of the information may or may not have the same understanding of the subject.

So, what are powerful questions? Powerful questions are those questions that help you get a deeper understanding of the subject. To get that understanding you need to learn something from your childhood. Showing a 4-year-old something is always challenging. Do they say, "Yes I understand"? That is highly unlikely; they want to know more, they ask lots of questions, who, what, why, where, when, and how. Just when you think you have answered all the questions', they come up with more. The reason the child does this is that they are curious. Our curiosity is a trait that we are all gifted with in our early years as we experience new things. However, the ability to be curious diminishes over time as our mind starts to revert to past experiences.

By being curious about the subject, person or group we are with we will start to open up all kinds of avenues that we were unaware of, which will lead to a far deeper understanding. If you are driving a discussion, you should actively encourage questions. If no questions are forthcoming, make sure you have a few of your own that will get the ball rolling.

Questions demonstrating Curiosity

Descriptive questions are used to dig a little deeper into the subject. Such questions will cause the person to think, so give them time.

Typical descriptive questions are:

Could you elaborate further?

Tell me more about that.

Could you help me understand?

I'm curious about

Curiosity is the key to any conversation. If you bare this in mind, you will get a greater understanding of what the person is saying. Being curious is the key to understanding the person or people with you are speaking.

Thought-provoking questions

By challenging the person's assumptions, you will start to peel back the layers of the topic under discussion. Few people stop to think about how their assumptions affect the decisions they make which are based on their values, belief system and bias. By questioning assumptions, you will be asking people to reflect on their values. Be careful not to be aggressive when doing this. By their very definition peoples' values and beliefs are very personal to them. However, assumptions are what stops progress. Assumptions are not facts. However, by assuming the result of any action people will stop or avoid that action.

Here are some questions that will challenge peoples' assumptions:

- How did you make that assumption?
- What if it was false?
- What might happen if you opted for a different course of action?
- How can you validate that assumption as truth?
- What led you to that conclusion?
- What can you do differently?
- What if you tried a different approach?

Getting your team or your peers to buy into your ideas will depend on how you demonstrate your interest in their issues. There are many types of questions that you could use. Examples of these are:

Clarification Questions

What do you mean?

Would that help meet the deadline?

How does that help?

Perspective Questions

Getting an agreed perspective on the conversation shows that you have been attentive. Some examples would be:

How does this idea fit into the project?

If we were to go ahead would this save us any time?

Would this help us reach our quota sooner?

How important is this to you in the larger scheme of things?

Open-ended questions

Open-ended questions are the most empowering questions that give the person you are speaking to space to reflect. It is important when you ask open questions that you give the person time to think through what you have just asked; the longer the pause, the more thinking has been done, which is a good thing. Most of the open-ended questions begin with What, When, How, Where, and When.

Here are some examples:

What:

What is the most challenging aspect of that?

What would be the best outcome?

What is the impact of what you have discovered?

What will make the most significant impact?

What would you do?

Where / When:

From where do you anticipate the highest resistance?

Where do you think you will be in 3 years?

When do you think you will finish?

When will we be able to demonstrate the ...?

How:

How will you measure the success of this?

How will you communicate this to the stakeholders?

Who:

Who will be directly affected?

Who else has provided you with feedback?

The world is full of people who have different opinions on many topics. You often hear people who are only too willing to express their point of view. As discussed, there is a natural response when we hear someone that has a different view of a topic than we do. That is to stop listening and to start to defend our position. When we combine Active Listening with Powerful Questions, we will demonstrate to everybody that we are interested in them and the subject under discussion. Being able to use these skills does require effort. However, it like everything else that is worthwhile; you need to practice.

Chapter 9

Writing

As a leader, people judge all your communication. Therefore, you need to be very careful when committing your thoughts and opinions in writing.

In business one of the primary ways of communicating is through writing. There are lots of methods that we use to express our ideas such as, reports, emails, texts, instant messaging, presentation slides, and memos. Although, memos are being used less frequently now.

Writing is something we take for granted and it is one of the main ways your colleagues, customers and potential customers judge you. What do you think when you spot a website with both spelling mistakes and grammatical errors? It is natural to have doubts about the credibility of the company behind the site. If they can't take their time to have a quality website how will they be able to ensure that their products or services are of the quality that you expect?

When you are writing

There are five distinct types of writing; expository, descriptive, narrative, persuasive, and creative. Each of these has a specific use in the business world, which style you use depends on the type of work you are doing and the audience that you are seeking to engage. For example, you should avoid a creative style when you are trying to persuade your audience to purchase your products or services.

- Expository
  Textbooks use the expository style; it is used to inform, explain, describe and define a subject.
- Descriptive
  This style is used in advertising when you describe the subject by painting pictures with words.
- Narrative
  This style is in use in autobiographies and fictional writing. It is where you put yourself into your characters shoes.
- Persuasive
  Persuasive writing is another style that can is in use in advertising. The difference from the descriptive method is that this is bias and contains opinions.
- Creative
  This style is when you want to provoke your readers' thoughts and challenge their current beliefs. It is also used to entertain and is in none fiction writing. The best thing about creative writing is that when you start you don't necessarily know where you are going to end.

Whatever style you use the language you use is imperative. The next time you write a report, try reading it as the recipient of the document. Is the language precise? We often write in vague terms, which can lead to the reader misunderstanding some of the details in your piece of work.

When writing in business, always consider these four essential factors and adopt an appropriate tone that reflects them all:

- Your status
- The reader's status
- Your relationship with the reader
- The content of the message

The tone you use in writing is fundamental. Remember, when we speak to someone around 30% of communication is through the sound of our voice.

Tone refers to the style or manner of expression you use, in your speech or writing. Just like in a conversation, the mood you use in your writing affects the way a reader interprets and responds to your message. The tone you choose in your document should be guided by whom you want to read the material, why you want them to understand it, and what reaction you hope to get.

In all business writing, you should strive for an overall tone that is confident, conversational, positive, and courteous.

- Confident tone: This conveys authority and helps assure the reader your message is important enough to warrant attention.
- Conversational tone: It's much better to use a more conversational tone today rather than the stilted, highly formal wording from the past. Write in a natural style, similar to how you speak. Avoid official language or dense jargon.
- Positive tone: Always look for positive ways to put across a message wherever possible, with the focus on benefits and strengths.
- Courteous tone: Aim to be polite and respectful to your audience. Avoid lecturing the reader or using language that suggests the reader is at fault or unreasonable. It's essential that what you write will not offend the reader.

Tone Refers To The Style Or Manner Of Expression You Use, https://www.coursehero.com/file/p44n671/Tone-refers-to-the-style-or-manner-of-exercise (accessed March 31, 2019).

The use of emails is endemic in today's world. It is incredible the way people have started to use different language and grammar when they write emails. The critical thing to remember is that once the email is sent, it is in the public domain. While communicating by email is quick and easy, the rules that apply when writing a report also apply to emails. Here are a few things that you should consider when writing an email:

- Never write an email if you are upset or angry
- Write a meaningful Subject Title
- Be Polite
- Be Precise
- Be Specific
- Make your message logical
- Make your message short
- Use short paragraphs
- Will the email get the results you are expecting?
- Would you be okay with someone forwarding the email?
- Always read your email twice before sending it
- Always check any attachment before you publish it
- Would a telephone call or a meeting be more appropriate?

You should also consider the device that people are likely to read the message on. Many people read emails on a mobile device such as a tablet or mobile phone. If you send a lengthy, detailed report to someone who is reading it on their mobile phone, it may not have the impact that you were expecting.

Social Media

If you have a social media page such as Facebook, LinkedIn or Instagram for either personal or business use treat them the same, with respect. Remember your friends, business colleagues, customers, prospective customers, and competition can, and often do, review everything you have written or wherever you have appeared. There is a tendency to relax when you are posting something from a personal perspective. However, be careful the videos and pictures that you post of that great party or holiday will be viewed by people that will try to use them in a negative context. The main thing to remember with social media is that once your opinion is made public, it is there forever. There have been cases where somebody's views that were written many years earlier were used to create a negative impression of them and their company.

Whether you text regularly, use Facebook, Instagram or any other internet application that allows you to communicate with many people at the same time, the rules are the same, whether for formal business reasons or that of a personal nature.

- Make sure you complete the profile of each application you intend to post in before you start to post. While each application will request similar information, don't cut and paste the data from one application to another.
- There are good and bad times to post. Generally posting things early in the morning is seen by fewer people. Posting things late in the morning or early afternoon get the best results. You can post things during the weekend, particularly on Facebook as this is when most people react to posts they have received.
- Consider using software that will schedule your posts. There are many applications on the web that allows you to write a post and then schedule it for a later time or day. Scheduling is great if you want to post something at the same time each week. You can spend an hour putting together all your posts for the week and then use the application to schedule them.
- People tend to believe that they should only post things when they have something to say. However, if you find an article that is relevant to your audience post it, this is a

powerful way of demonstrating that you are a thought leader.

- Don't just publish texts use video's as well. While texts are an excellent way to get your message across the use of video's will attract more followers, in fact, social media companies actively encourage it. You don't need a Hollywood blockbuster, using your smartphone to record a video can be very useful.
- As more people read your posts, you will start to get comments. Always respond to the comments. If you have too many comments seek out the questions and answer those first, then the complaints.
- Don't ignore negative comments or complaints. While people look at all your posts, they will inevitably be drawn to the negative comments and criticisms. How you respond can enhance your reputation, or it could be a public relations disaster. If people have a complaint treat it with respect, try to answer in a positive tone and leave a number or email address that they can call to resolve their issue.
- Make sure all the posts that you send are from you. Don't ask someone to post on your behalf. Your reputation can and will be adversely affected, and people that will see your message will assume that they come from your values. Having someone send messages on your behalf will be spotted, and if they don't have the same values as yourself, this can lead to a disastrous situation.
- Remember that while you are using social media to sell your products and services don't be too pushy. Use sales media to educate and inform people about your products and services. You can use the Facebook Business page to link to your website where prospective customers can purchase your goods and services.

The main thing is to remember that social media is an excellent way of communicating with many people. However, before you press that post button remember:

- Never post anything in anger
- Be careful what you write
- Be Polite
- Be Precise
- Be Specific
- Make your message logical
- Read everything twice before you post it
- Then read it again
- Read it out loud
- Imagine your best prospect/CEO/competition reading it

Social media is something that is being used by businesses more and more often. When used correctly social media can be a compelling way of communicating your ideas, opinions and successes. Just treat it with respect.

Chapter 10

Mindfulness

In this chapter, we will look at two things Mindfulness and Meditation. The reason for that is Meditation will help free your mind of the internal chatter that we all have, and Mindfulness will help you focus on the tasks you need to complete.

Mindfulness

What is Mindfulness? Why is it something worth considering in a working environment? Isn't this the latest fad? These questions are asked regularly.

Leading people can be a challenge as so many people, whether they are part of your team, colleagues, customers or potential customers, will want your attention. It is difficult to focus on any one question or issue when you have so many things that are going on around you. So how do you cope? One way is to use the Mindfulness technique. It is important to realise that using Mindfulness is something that you choose to do in specific circumstances. Being pushed into a situation or where you feel you do not have enough time is an ideal time to use the Mindfulness technique.

Have you heard the phrase "If you always do what you always did, you will always get what you always got." Well, that is what happens to most of us. Humans are creatures of habit, and as such we tend to repeat the same actions, again and again, no matter what the result. What is perplexing is that we repeat the same actions even if they were unsuccessful. Using Mindfulness techniques will help you break out of this cycle.

Firstly, let's look at what Mindfulness is. There are many variations and lots of ways to practice Mindfulness, but the basic definition of Mindfulness is "being able to live in the present, being able to appreciate what is happening around you fully, and in your mind, at any given point in time and make decisions on the facts presented to you." If you want to experience the power of Mindfulness the next time you have a meal try focusing on each mouthful that you eat, explore the texture, the taste, and how this makes you feel. Make sure you have finished that mouthful before you look at your plate for your next choice. The result is that you enjoy your meal and taste and enjoy it for, probably, the first time in a long time.

Our mind is remarkable as it processes between 40,000 and 60,000 thoughts every day. These thoughts focus mainly on the past, checking how our current activity matches what we have experienced in the past. These thoughts are looking for help from our prior experiences. However, to cope with so many ideas, the brain passes most decisions to the subconscious. Therefore, there are occasions when we have driven home, and we wonder how we got there. While we were thinking of the more important daily activities which occupied the frontal lobe of our brain, the subconscious took over the driving of the car. The only time we would have realised what was happening would be if something unusual had happened or something that needed our attention had suddenly become apparent.

The same process happens in our daily life. We make subconscious decisions where we have experience of a similar situation. The conscious brain only becomes aware of the issue when we come across a situation that we have not experienced before. As an example, when you meet someone you are familiar with you will have an opinion of them which means you will automatically see them in a good or bad light. In a work environment you may feel apprehensive just before writing a report, the apprehension is most likely the result of a bad experience in the past.

Our belief system and values are helping us pass judgement. These beliefs and judgements are something that we learnt from our community, parents, teachers and peers and so we assess any decision we make against what we believe to be true. However, is our view of the world, always right? Can other people have a different view of the world which is just as legitimate as ours? In today's business environment leaders are expected to work with people from different cultures and up to five generations each of these groups will have a different view of numerous subjects and each opinion could be legitimate.

Mindfulness is making an important decision as if it was the first time you had to make that decision. It is being aware that you are about to make an "automatic decision" and then reassessing the facts to ensure you are making the correct decision at that moment.

It is not possible to use Mindfulness in every decision we make. Do I take milk in my coffee? What coffee should I have? Do I take sugar in my coffee? What size cup should I use? What colour should the cup be? However, there are decisions we make every day which would benefit from assessing all the facts without referring to past decisions.

How do we practice Mindfulness? There are two things you need to do. The first is to choose which areas you want to practice the technique and the second is to commit to using Mindfulness. To select the subjects, you intend to focus on, start by writing your daily tasks down. One form of this would be a "To Do List". This list will have jobs and actions that you need to complete today. Which of these are essential and would have the most significant impact on your company's or your goals? Put a star against all the tasks and actions that would have a considerable effect. Now when you are looking to decide on an action start by looking at all the facts. As an example, will senior management receive your report? Have you assessed the impact of the report recently? Do you gather the same data and statistics and update them? Alternatively, do you take a more in-depth look at what you are writing? Are you writing too much information or too little? Where do you get your data from, are there other areas that you could access data? Are you presenting your report without any bias? Can you justify the prejudice in your report?

Many people use To-Do lists to help them prioritise their daily tasks. To-Do lists are a great method to ensure you don't forget what jobs you have yet to complete. The issue is that To Do lists are just that – a list. How important is each task to you, your team or your company? Is it helping you to move to your goal? Very few people write down and commit to their goals; it is about 1%. What is extraordinary is that most of the hugely successful people use a goal setting methodology. So, if you want to be successful, the obvious thing is to start writing your goals down then break them down into smaller tasks, then break down those tasks to subtasks as was detailed in Chapter 4 Goal Setting. The subtasks should be no more than 60 minutes in length and preferably around 30 minutes. Why does this help in Mindfulness? Because then you can focus on that individual task or subtask and know that it is helping you drive to your goal. Many people talk about multi-tasking, but that is a myth. You can only give your full attention to one task at a time. While the subconscious part of your mind will work on tasks, it is only capable of repeating past actions and decisions. That is why so many people are running on autopilot.

Meditation

Mindfulness is a conscious decision to look at everyday tasks in a different way. One of the ways to teach yourself to use Mindfulness and "be in the moment" is to meditate. That does not mean locking yourself away in a retreat for years and searching for the meaning of life; you need about 10 minutes a day. Many gurus can teach you how to meditate and get the best from your experience. However, if you are new to meditation, there is a fundamental process that you can use. There are just three steps:

1. Sit upright in a chair. Posture is important when you start to meditate
2. Close your eyes. Stopping all visual images lets you shut out the outside world
3. Focus on your breathing. Breathe in for a count of 3, breathe out for a count of 5. Just breath in and out and focus on each breath. Your mind will begin to roam, let it, but then bring it back by focusing on your breathing. Another technique is to breathe in for a count of 4 and then breathe out for a count of four, that is one breath. Repeat these breaths 20 times. However, if you miss count and let your mind wander, you must start over again.

When you start, it would be advisable to use an app to let you know when your time has elapsed. However, once you have more experience meditating you will be able to imagine a clock in your mind and then set a time when you want to stop meditating when the time elapses you will start to "come to". You may be sceptical at this ability, but many people use it very successfully. It is amazing how this simple process will help reduce stress and anxiety.

There is a science behind meditation. The brain is an electrochemical organ, and as such generates electrical power in the form of brain waves. The brain has four distinct states which are:

- Beta
  Beta activity creates brain waves from 15 to 40 cycles per second. When we are fully awake and are focusing on a task, we will be in this state

- Alpha
  Alpha is when we have completed the task and are relaxing. The brain waves that are dominant range from 9 to 14 cycles per second
- Theta
  When we have achieved a task and start to unwind by staring into space or go for a walk, we enter this state. The Theta is the state we are trying to achieve when we meditate. The dominant brain wave ranges from 5 to 8 cycles per second.
- Delta
  When we enter a deep sleep stage, our brain activity falls and so does the dominant brain waves. These brain waves range from 1.5 to 4 cycles per second.

The Theta stage is where we are at our best from a creative perspective. It is in this stage where ideas flow. They are not filtered or judged.

That is the theory. Now, imagine your next primary task. If you could spend 10 minutes focusing on that task and allowing your mind to consider many options, without judgment, you would inevitably start to format ideas that you had not thought of before.

Mediation will help you clear your mind of all the internal chatter that we all have. You may gain some insight into the tasks you have to complete. The critical point is that you have stopped and cleared your mind so that you can now concentrate on the task list that you have in front of you. Look at the most critical task. How does it make you feel? Have you done the task before? What happened the last time you did a task like this? If you feel excited about the opportunity, then start to write down how you are going to complete the task. Be as detailed as you can. Focus on the processes that you will need to go through.

If the task you are thinking about gives you an uneasy feeling, then start to explore why you feel uneasy. What happened the last time you completed this or a similar task? Are you concerned about other peoples' reaction to the task, or are you worried about the time it will take? Are you communicating with people that you find challenging? Explore your feelings. Now ask if the thing you are concerned about is essential if it is then looking at how you can change the circumstances.

In most cases, the uneasy feeling is an attitude of your mind. By exploring what has made you uncomfortable, you will either determine that your past experiences are no longer relevant, or you will become aware of the knowledge that is making you feel uneasy.

Both Meditation and Mindfulness are not fads or something new; many civilisations have used them throughout history. They are a way of connecting with how you are feeling in the present and will help you make far better decisions, achieve your goals and be far more productive.

Chapter 11

Stress

As a leader, it is crucial that you manage your stress, but it is also essential to recognise and help members of your team cope with their stress.

Stress and the response to stress happens to us all, every day. From getting up and finding that there is no milk, driving to work and finding that the traffic is much heavier than usual. Then getting to work and discovering that your email inbox has lots of urgent requests, being too busy for lunch, meetings have been arranged and cancelled, driving home in the rain, you forgot to put the cat out before you left, you burn your dinner, and you started watching a film when the broadband link went down. No wonder you are stressed.

Pressure Performance Curve

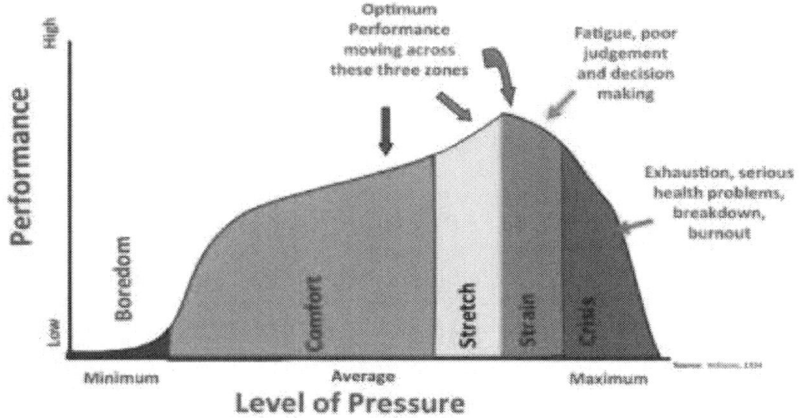

As the diagram above shows stress or pressure can be useful for us. The issue is when your stress response doesn't have time to go back to normal. When that happens, and you suffer from stress regularly many times a day you can start to suffer from chronic stress, and that is very bad for you.

Work-related stress is widespread. However, what is stress? Why is some stress good for you? Have you ever been involved in a presentation that you had to give? If so, you no doubt felt nervous before you started, did you feel your heart racing, did your palms sweat? Were you tense? That is stress. One of the benefits of stress is that you become more focused which means you will react quicker and think quicker than usual. By being more focused and reacting quicker means, you can quickly assess the issue you are confronted with and deal with it appropriately.

Stress is generally based on two things being under threat or fear. But, what are those fears? Examples are fear of being late, fear of not being in control, fear of being wrong, and the big one fear of failure.

In the past when your ancestors faced a threat, and they became fearful it was because their life was in imminent danger and so part of their brain, the hypothalamus, sent out an order to the body to be prepared for "fight, flight or freeze". That instruction released the stress hormones adrenaline and cortisol which caused the heart to beat faster and send more blood to the areas that were needed in emergencies such as the heart, muscles and other vital organs. The release of adrenalin and cortisol prepared the body to make a quick getaway or to fight. Once the issue that caused the stress had gone away, the Central Nervous System informed the hypothalamus that everything is okay, and the instruction was sent out to stop sending the stress hormones.

Now fast forward to the present day. You are in a position where you are worried that you will be late for a meeting and the closer to the time of the meeting the more you realise that you won't be on time. Unfortunately, the brain does not have a mechanism for late meetings! Instead, the situation is deemed a threat, and the hypothalamus goes into action. The next time you are going to be late for a meeting you should check your response. Is your heart racing, are you starting to perspire? Do you feel tense? If one or more of those happen, you are under stress. The critical thing to understand is that the mind reacts to a "perceived" threat. While the danger maybe important it is not life or death.

When we are continually bombarded with information which demands that we make a decision and our brain sees this as a threat and starts the stress cycle. The stress cycle starts because the mind has a way of coping with decisions that occur regularly; it passes the decision to the subconscious part of the brain. That means when you come across a situation where you have reacted before the subconscious makes the same decision that was made based on that experience. The result is that if you felt stressed over a task in the past, you are going to feel stressed about that situation from then on. However, you can break this circle. The way to do that is to question yourself when you start to feel stressed, why am I feeling this way? Analyse what you fear because that is what is causing you to feel stressed. In most situations when you start to realise that there is nothing to fear in the task or project you will start to feel under control. Chapter 10 on Mindfulness describes how you can use Mindfulness and Meditation to relieve stress.

Some mental issues we face when we have too much stress are mental cloudiness, headaches, irritability, anxiety, depression and insomnia. Stress also takes its toll on the body which results in weight gain, high blood pressure, a weakened immune system, digestive problems, a reduced sex drive, heart disease, stomach ache and tense muscles. If you are taking medication for high blood pressure, have digestive issues such as heartburn or lots of indigestion and suffer from headaches and a bad back you need to look for a way to reduce your stress levels. The good news is that you can.

There are numerous ways to manage stress.

1. Realise what is happening to you

   The first and most important thing is to realise what is happening. Remember that the brain is reacting to a "perceived" threat. If you are not in imminent bodily danger, then assess why you believe you are in danger. What is making you react the way you are? As you convince yourself that the danger is not real, you will start to become calmer.

2. Meditate

   Meditation can help reduce stress levels. The best time to meditate is early in the morning before the daily activity starts. Take a few minutes to focus on your breathing and begin to imagine a perfect day. What would that be? How would that feel? Who would be involved on your ideal day? Be careful that you don't drift off to sleep as this can be very relaxing.

Remember that while you are visualising a perfect day, it is unlikely to happen as you imagined.

Some people meditate during lunch which can help recharge your batteries.

You can also meditate later in the day, which can also be beneficial as there is a strong likelihood that you will drift off to sleep, which will help you if you have insomnia.

3. Use a Goal Setting system

As described in Chapter 4 Goal Setting writing down what you need to do that day will help relieve stress. By writing what you need to do you stop worrying about things you might have forgotten. However, to take control, you should go a little further than creating a To Do List. Try using a Goal Setting program as described in Chapter 4. The first thing to do is some self-analysis, write down what is important to your Company and yourself. Look at different aspects of your work such as Internal Relationships, External Relationships, Finance, Management, Education, Projects, Rest and Relaxation, Health and Fitness. Then write down five goals that you want to achieve. The next step is the most important, break down those goals into small manageable tasks. As an example, if you need to write a Business Plan break down the goal by chapters. Breaking down the primary goals to small bite-size chunks makes any major project look achievable.

Don’t forget to review your tasks and the beginning and end of each day.

4. Exercise

   Exercise is one of the best ways to rest your system. Exercise helps the body and mind. Exercising doesn't mean joining a gym and having a strenuous 2-hour workout. You can gain a great deal from using the stairs in the office rather than taking the lift. Try parking the car away from the office and walking the rest of the way, or getting off the train, tube or bus a couple of stops early and walking. In other words, any exercise is right for you. Once you get into the habit of exercising you will start to see the benefits from both your mind and body.

5. Maintain a healthy diet

   One of the possible outcomes of too much stress is eating too much and therefore putting on weight. You will find yourself eating sweet snacks to give you a “sugar boost”. Fast food or eating at your desk becomes the norm. If you need to eat at your desk, then have a piece of fruit rather than a chocolate bar. Remember fresh food is better than processed food. By eating a healthy diet, you are replenishing all those vitamins that you lose when you are stressed.

6. Reduce consumption of caffeine and alcohol

   Reducing consumption doesn't mean abstaining from either caffeine or alcohol; it just means be aware of how much you are drinking. We can get into a habit of going to the coffee machine when we come across a problem. Alcohol is great in social situations but as has been documented many times too much alcohol can lead to serious health issues.

7. Aim for 7 to 8 hours of sleep a night

   One of the things that happen when we are under stress is that you worry at night. When it seems you cannot get to sleep there are some great ways to help. Remember don't drink caffeine or alcohol before getting ready for bed, try reading before bed rather than watching tv, and have a glass of warm milk. If you have started meditation try relaxing when you get into bed by using the same technique. Finally, stop worrying about not getting enough sleep, it is a vicious circle because the more you worry, the less likely you are to sleep and the less rest you are getting, the more you worry.

8. Stay socially connected

   Having a good social life helps relax you. By mixing with people and sharing their experiences, your stress levels will start to reduce. In our society loneliness is something that many people deal with every day. What are your interests? Is there a local club that you could join that caters to your interest?

9. Make time for rest and relaxation

   Many people feel guilty if they spend time relaxing and enjoying themselves while there is so much to do. Believe it or not, this is one of the best things you can do to reduce your stress levels. Set a regular time for yourself to chill out. Do something you enjoy, play games on the internet, read, complete some puzzles, meet friends.

10. Seek help from your doctor

    You should always remember that if the stress gets too much that the doctor will help. Some medications will help you start the journey to a calmer you. However, pills aren't the final answer; they are a way to help you get started. Then look at your lifestyle and commit to change.

Stress happens to us all, and we all need stress to help us grow. However, too much stress is bad and can lead to health and relationship problems. Remember our brain reacts to perceived threats the more we realise this, the greater chance we have in controlling our responses.

Chapter 12

Work, Rest and Play

Looking after yourself as a leader is vital to ensure you are making the right decisions and creating the right opportunities for your team. However, it is just as important that you are aware of your team's overall health. If you notice that the team is struggling, maybe there is something you could implement to ensure that they are mentally and physically exercised. Alternatively, at least make them aware of the benefits discussed in this chapter. Make sure that where possible your team are given and taking breaks and finding time to relax. There will be some weeks where your team needs to put in that extra mile in, but make sure that any extra effort is rewarded, and you ensure the team has time to rest later.

Business life today is, generally, fast-paced and demanding. The demands are constant whether that is from your board, senior managers, team members, customers, or potential customers. They are all demanding both your time and knowledge, and this is how it should be; let's face it if nobody wanted to speak to you there would be a legitimate question regarding your value to the company. The issue is that we constantly battle with the "work-life balance". Some people feel that they need to put the hours in because they are in fear of being overlooked for promotion or losing their jobs. In some companies, it is the usual practice to start early and work late. Indeed, because of technology we are never out of reach. Our business life constantly interrupts our personal experience. While this may well demonstrate that you are an invaluable member of the organisation, is it healthy? Are you leading your team or are you setting a bad example?

Helping your company to be successful is very rewarding. Being part of a successful team is equally satisfying, and sometimes business dictates that we should go the extra mile. The issue is when going the extra mile becomes the norm because when we are working so hard, we become stressed. Eventually, the stress level can overwhelm us unless we take time out to rest and relax.

Have you ever heard the saying "all work and no play, makes Jack a dull boy." Well, it turns out that is only half the story. All work and no play is detrimental to both your physical and mental health. You can understand how sitting all day can affect your physical health, but your mental health can be severely affected if you don't give your mind time to recover. So, the same rules should apply to your body and mind. Exercise both regularly and give both your mind and body time to heal each day.

There have been many studies in the past that have shown that regular exercise is beneficial. There is also growing evidence that regular exercise is beneficial to your mental health. On top of that exercising your mind is vital if you want to have the opportunity to reach your full potential.

When we discuss exercise, you often hear people say they have not got enough time. The fact is that everybody has the same amount of time. Time is constant. Therefore time cannot be the issue. The real question is one of your priorities. What do you prioritise in your everyday life? Do you prioritise an extra hour in bed, or watching television for three hours a night? We all have a choice to make concerning exercise, and that is, do we want to engage in physical and mental exercise or not?

Physical Exercise

There are plenty of studies that show moderate physical exercise will help reduce the chance of heart disease, stroke, and diabetes. It also helps you lose weight and lower your blood pressure and relieve the daily stress that builds up in all of us. However, did you know that physical exercise also helps dramatically improve your mental health? Studies have shown that regular aerobic exercise, the kind that gets your heart and your sweat glands pumping, appears to boost the size of the hippocampus, the brain area involved in verbal memory and learning. Exercise helps your memory through both direct and indirect means. The benefits of exercise come directly from its ability to reduce insulin resistance, reduce inflammation, and stimulate the release of growth factors, which are chemicals in the brain that affect the health of brain cells, the growth of new blood vessels in the brain, and even the abundance and survival of new brain cells. Many studies have suggested that the parts of the brain that control thinking and memory (the prefrontal cortex and medial temporal cortex) have greater volume in people who exercise versus people who don't.

Indirectly, exercise improves mood and sleep and reduces stress and anxiety. Problems in these areas frequently cause or contribute to cognitive impairment.

Regular Exercise Changes The Brain - Harvard Health Blog, https://www.health.harvard.edu/blog/regular-exercise-changes-brain-improve-memory accessed March 31, 2019.

There are not many successful leaders that do not exercise regularly. If you think about it most leaders today seem reasonably fit, in that, they are neither overweight or obese. There is a great deal of expectation placed on leaders today. Leaders are expected to be able to make decisions at any time of the day, and you can only make informed choices if you can entirely focus on the issue at hand. If you are not fit it is likely you will be tired at the end of the day, which means that decisions made at the end of the day will be open to question.

Committing to physical exercise does not mean joining a gym and having a daily 1-hour workout, while that may be something that will benefit some people; it is not for everybody. Committing to physical exercise may mean that you will go for a 10-minute walk in the morning, at lunchtime or in the evening. It might also suggest that you will use the stairs rather than the lift, or you will get off the tube or bus a couple of steps further away from your place of work. The point is that you will be committing to exercising more now than in the past. Try using a plan to steadily increase in your physical activity and use the Goal Setting method, as described in Chapter 4, to achieve this. The recommended level of exercise to help both physical and mental health is around 120 minutes per week.

There are many people who at New Year have a resolution "to get fit". However, what does that mean? What is fit? A far better way would be to state a weight that you want to be, a dress size you want to fit into, or a waist size you want. These are all SMART (Specific, Measurable, Achievable, Relevant, Time-bound) Goals. Remember to tell everybody what you have committed to because when you are struggling people around you will help.

Your Mind

Exercising your mind is just as important as exercising your body. Regularly using your mind will help you reduce stress, be calmer, and be able to be far more creative when problem-solving. Very few people allocate a regular time for exercising their mind. However, it is imperative if you want the chance to reach your full potential. We are all bombarded with information every minute of every day. Your mind is constantly processing this information and coming to decisions or conclusions every second.

The brain is made up of neurons and synapses, and it is how these connect that helps our mental agility. Also, when our mind gets tired our mind begins to wander, and our attention span reduces dramatically. Research has shown that people who have a greater attention span make far better decisions based on facts. Those people whose mind is fatigued tend to make decisions based on emotions, which can be very unpredictable. By working on the problem-solving puzzles, your brain will start to develop new connections. There are many such puzzles online, and a lot are free to use. Have you tried a Sudoku challenge, or a crossword, or a word game? The next time you have free time don't stare at the television, try working on a puzzle instead.

What is mental exercise? There are two types the first is solving puzzles, and the second is meta-thinking or thinking about thinking which is best done while meditating which is explained in Chapter 10 Mindfulness. There are proven ways that you can exercise your mind they include word games, number puzzles, reading a book, learning a musical instrument, learning a language, in fact learning anything new is of benefit as it creates different pathways in your brain.

How much time should you allocate each day to exercising your mind? If the same question were asked about the physical exercise, you would know that you will need to start slowly and build up. Exercising your mind is the same. If you aim for 45 minutes a day, it will be like getting up and trying to run a half marathon when you are not physically fit. You will need to plan how you will get to 45 minutes per day. The best way would be to allocate 15 minutes a day for the first week and then in the second week add 10 minutes, 10 minutes in the third week and 10 minutes in the fourth week. You should pick a time that suits you, one that you can commit to each day.

Brain exercise requires commitment, but it is also one that might give you the most benefit. Researchers believe that the most effective brain training exercises are those that are challenging, novel and complex. Learning something new is one way to keep your brain on its toes so continually introducing new challenges will help improve the brains capability.

In one study a researcher assigned older adults to learn a variety of new skills ranging from digital photography to quilting. They then did a series of memory tests and compared the experimental groups to control groups. Those in the control groups had engaged in activities that were fun but not mentally challenging such as watching movies and listening to the radio. The researchers found that only those participants who had learned a new skill experienced improvement on the memory tests. They also discovered that these memory improvements were still present when tested again a year later.

5 Brain Exercises To Strengthen Your Mind, https://www.verywellmind.com/brain-exercises-to-strengthen-your-mind-2795039 (accessed March 31, 2019).

So have fun learning a new skill.

Rest

We all realise that we have physical limitations and that when we reach those limitations, it is time to rest, so why do so many people neglect to rest when they have reached their mental limit. A tired mind is unpredictable, you find it difficult to focus, and some of the decisions you make will be questionable when you review them. How many people do you know that are grumpy when they are tired? That is because the mind needs time to rest.

To ensure you are at your peak, you should be aware of three states of your mind, which are resting, relaxing and sleep.

Resting is when you stop what you are doing and allow your mind to wander, or listen to the radio, or you pick up a book or have a chat with a friend. If you have a regular time when you switch off for 10 or 15 minutes, you will give your mind time to reset, and file all that data that you have been focusing on during your daily activities.

Relaxing Is when you entirely switch off from your worries and concerns. If you participate in a sport or enjoy reading a good book, or sit back and watch television for an hour, or daydream. The point is to "forget" about the everyday issues that we all face. By doing this regularly your mind is slowing down, that is why so many people fall asleep in front of the television, fatigue overtakes them.

Sleep is essential and having a regular sleep pattern is one of the most important things you can do to have a stable and creative mind. The current wisdom is that you should sleep between 6 and 8 hours each night. By having a regular sleep pattern, your brain will complete all the activities that are vital to ensure it is healthy. Also, our bodies have time to relax and repair those aching muscles.

Being a leader is challenging and demanding and so looking after your physical and mental health is vital. So here a few suggestions to keep you fit:

- Exercise for at least 120 minutes a week
- Read books and articles that are outside your current knowledge
- Complete a word and/or number puzzle that challenges you at least once per day
- Learn a new activity
- Rest for at least 15 minutes, three times per day
- Relax for at least an hour each day
- Have a regular sleep pattern

Therefore, for you and your team to be productive be aware when it is time to work, time to rest, time to relax and time for fun.

References

"Maslow's Hierarchy Of Needs | Simply Psychology."

www.16personalities.com

"The Peter Principle" by Peter and Raymond Hull

The Definitive Book of Body Language – Alan and Barbara Pease

Grinder and Bandler and is known as Neuro-linguistic Programming or NLP

Wheel Of Life Paul J. Meyer, founder of Success Motivation® Institute, Inc.

Regular Exercise Changes The Brain To Improve Memory Retrieved from https://www.health.harvard.edu/blog/regular-exercise-changes-brain-improve-memory

The Neurological Benefits Of Exercise - Positive Psychology. (n.d.). Retrieved from https://positivepsychologyprogram.com/exercise-neurological-benefits

Tone Refers To The Style Or Manner Of Expression You Use .., https://www.coursehero.com/file/p44n671/Tone-refers-to-the-style-or-manner-of-exercise (accessed March 31, 2019).

Become A Better Listener: Active Listening - Psych Central, https://psychcentral.com/lib/become-a-better-listener-active-listening (accessed March 31, 2019).

The Myers & Briggs Foundation - Mbti® Basics, https://www.myersbriggs.org/my-mbti-personality-type/mbti-basics (accessed March 31, 2019).

I NEED YOU
to hate me

I NEED YOU BOOK ONE

GENICIOUS

Special Edition

ISBN: 978-0-6454792-9-4

https://genicious.com